# The Best Fit:

# Creating the Right LRE for Your Students with Special Needs

By Barbara F. Zimmerman, Ph.D.

LRP Publications

LRP Publications
Horsham, Pennsylvania 19044

This publication was designed to provide accurate and authoritative information in regard to the subject matter covered. It is published with the understanding that neither the author nor the publisher is engaged in rendering legal, accounting, or other professional service. If legal advice or other expert assistance is required, the service of a competent professional should be sought.

**Library of Congress Cataloging-in-Publication Data**

Zimmerman, Barbara F.
    The best fit : creating the right LRE for your students with special needs / Barbara F. Zimmerman.
        p.    cm.
    Includes bibliographical references.
    ISBN 1-57834-031-4
    1.   Inclusive education.  I.   Title.

LC1200 .Z56   2002
371.9'046--dc21

2002072925

**For My Dad**

**Marvin D. Zimmerman**

**1926-2001**

**A wonderful father and an extraordinary educator**

# About the Author

**BARBARA ZIMMERMAN, Ph.D.,** was a special education teacher with the Capital Region BOCES for 12 years. Currently she works as a Behavior Specialist providing workshops and consultations on positive behavior management for school districts, parents and agencies that work with children. She has taught graduate courses in Emotional Disturbance and Behavior Disorders and Behavior Management at The College of St. Rose in Albany, New York.

Dr. Zimmerman has broad experience with disruptive behavior as a former "disrupter," a counselor and a teacher of disruptive students. She has worked with behaviorally disordered and emotionally disturbed children from the pre-school to the high school level. Additionally, Dr. Zimmerman spent two years working at St. Anne's Institute, a residential facility for emotionally disturbed teen-age girls. She also taught night college courses at New York State Prisons in Wilton and Hudson.

Dr. Zimmerman is a national speaker whose presentations and consultations include positive behavior management techniques for children and adolescents who exhibit disruptive behavior, as well as general and specific ideas on humane and positive management. Different teaching and management styles also are taken into consideration. Dr. Zimmerman believes that children and adults are all individuals who have different needs. She invites people to

**v**

actively participate in the workshops she presents, as she believes that we have much to teach each other.

Dr. Zimmerman is also the author of LRP Publications,' *On Our Best Behavior: Positive Behavior Management Strategies for the Classroom*, and *Why Can't They Just Behave: A Guide to Managing Student Behavior Disorders*.

# Table of Contents

# Acknowledgments

Many thanks to Jane Searle and Esther Willison who edited this book with great care. Their precision and creativity were invaluable. I also thank my editor from LRP Publications, Maria Neithercott, who is always wonderful to work with.

This book would not have been possible without the efforts of many individuals who assisted me in my research. Their willingness to share facts, events and experiences breathe life into this book. I am greatly appreciative of the following people: Judy Dyer, Lynn Goliber, Mitchell Goliber, Kelly Kissane, Dr. Wilma Jozwiak, Kathy Lupi, Karen Norlander, Esq., Faye Tischler, and Esther Willison.

I am in tremendous debt to Traci Housten-Harris, Elizabeth Heck, Dr. Reda Girgis, Dr. Fredrick Wigley and the other staff members of the Pulmonary Critical Care Unit at Johns Hopkins Medical Center, who keep me breathing. I give a special thank you to Spenser Scharfman who is my hero and role model. He has shown me the way to live life with a physical disability.

My work environment has always been a place of enlightenment and encouragement. I am grateful to all of my colleagues at the Capital Region Board of Cooperative Educational Services. In particular, I would like to thank Dr. Barbara Nagler, Dr. Inge Carmola, and Terry Tice. They have provided me with a work environment that enables me to do my work in the most comfortable and productive way possible.

Additionally I thank my life-long friends, Janet Fein, Joy and Stewart Scharfman, and Elinor and Mark Furman who are always there for me. I also thank Diana Rosen who reminds me of all the things that are important and all of the things that are not so important.

Without the emotional and physical support of many people I would not be able to do many things I love to do, most importantly, my work. Special thanks to Ellen Burns, Julie Magnano, Mary Leech, Marie Brander, Carron Rutnick, Cindy Neal, Jackie and Michael Foster, George Puzio, Jill Hannifan, Joan Schulz, Bonnie Spanier, Judy Fetterly, Susan Kaplow, and Lois Uttley.

I thank my mother, Natalie, and my brother, Ira and sister, Janie. I also thank Judith, my stepdaughter.

I thank the wonderful children and adolescents in my life who still, gratefully, laugh at my jokes and still play with me. Loving thoughts of Adam, Dana, Elise, Ellen, Laura, Lynnie, Mollie, Pini, Rivka and Spenser remain in my heart always.

Lastly, I thank Esther, my partner, who has always been everything. Now she is more than everything.

# Chapter One

# Introduction

This book will serve as a review of "least restrictive environment" (LRE) and inform educators of useful information needed to make decisions about when and how to mainstream and include identified students into general education schools and classrooms.

Clearly, in the last 20 years, inclusion and related topics have been the source of much controversy. Some of the controversy is due to misinformation. Some is a result of inadequate and inept preparation and implementation of mainstreaming and inclusionary programs. Research based on current educational theory and interviews with educators, parents and students, guide the information presented. The parent point of view is included in order to help educators work more effectively with the students they serve and with the parents of these students. (All names of those interviewd have been changed for purposes of confidentiality.) The appropriate and necessary supports for both teachers and students will be discussed extensively.

In 1981 I started my career as a special education teacher. When I applied for teaching positions in the public schools there were basically two types of special education programs. There was the resource room, where identified students with disabilities were

**1**

mainstreamed for a good portion of the day, approximately 50 to 95 percent of the time. These students were placed in the resource room in order to receive assistance, remediation and, in some instances, to receive some primary instruction in reading, math, science, writing, social studies or other academic subjects. For the rest of the day the mainstreamed students would go to general education classes to receive academic instruction. The other special education program available was the self-contained classroom. This educational setting was for students whose disabilities were deemed too overwhelming, either cognitively or behaviorally, for a general education program. In this setting, all of the students in the class had similar disabilities. Students in these classes received all of their academic, behavioral and social instruction in a segregated program.

I was fortunate to receive a teaching position in upstate New York working for the Board of Cooperative Educational Services (BOCES). All of the counties in New York State have access to a regional BOCES. If a district has one or two students at a certain age level with a specific disability the district is unable to accommodate, it can contract with BOCES. There are BOCES classrooms designed for specific disabilities at specific age levels that are housed in various local schools in the BOCES district. In this way, students can be accommodated in other schools or neighboring districts. Most often when students are placed in a BOCES program, they are not housed in their home school, and in many other cases they are not housed in their home school district. Other states have similar cooperative educational programs.

When I first started my teaching career most of the BOCES programs generally were self-contained classrooms, with limited opportunities for the students in those programs to mainstream into the general population. I did, however, make an effort to find general education teachers who would accept my students and many of my students did mainstream, and most of them were successful academically and socially. Some of my students went willingly; others had to be coaxed, and still others flatly refused. Inclusionary programs were just on the horizon, and many of the school districts began to take students, who had previously been placed in BOCES programs, back into their home school districts and in some cases back to the students' home schools. As each year passed, the student population in my BOCES self-contained classroom changed. Districts were only sending students who either had severe emotional/behavioral, developmental, and/or cognitive difficulties to out-of-district programs. My classroom accommodated students who had behavioral difficulties and each year the frequency and intensity of behavioral outbursts displayed by my students increased.

As I reflect on my 12 years of teaching in a self-contained program, I believe there were students who could have been totally and successfully included in the general education setting. This is particularly true for the

**3**

students I had at the beginning of my teaching career. I had other students who could have been successful in the inclusionary classroom environment with appropriate supports. Still other students may or may not have been successful with the same supports. I do believe, however, that there were many students I had in my class who would never have been successful in a totally inclusive educational program. This is due, to some extent, to the manner in which the inclusionary programs were set up.

For the past 11 years I have been a behavior specialist. I have seen students, identified and unidentified, who have struggled in the general education setting. I also have seen students with disabilities flourish in the general education setting. Many factors are involved in how well any student will do in any educational setting.

Regardless of what anyone believes about mainstreaming or inclusion, decisions for appropriate placement and appropriate services have to be made after careful consideration of each individual student. It is important to look at "the big picture." What are realistic expectations of this student now, and what can we reasonably predict for this student 10 years from now? Without this case-by-case consideration, the potential for failing the students with special needs increases dramatically. These are the students who, perhaps, most of all, depend on us to not fail them.

# Chapter Two

# Background and History

The movement to mainstream and include students with disabilities in this country has its roots in the early civil rights movement. "In 1954 the U.S. Supreme Court decision *Brown v. Board of Education of Topeka* ruled that school segregation violated the 14th Amendment, thus setting a precedent for equality, in education, for children with disabilities" (Wood 1992, p.7).

In 1975, the Education for All Handicapped Children Act (Public Law 94-142) was passed. Public Law 94-142 called for five major components that would affect the classroom and affect instruction: a right to a free appropriate public education (FAPE), nondiscriminatory evaluation procedures, procedural due process, individualized education programs (IEPs), and least restrictive environment (LRE).

The law guaranteed the right of every student with a disability to a *free appropriate public education*. Although many schools were serving some students with disabilities at that time, the landmark legislation ensured that no student, regardless of his or her disability, could be turned away by the public education system. "By law, all children are guaranteed a free appropriate public education at no expense to parents or guardians. Historically, many children with disabilities were denied this basic freedom; as a result, they received no education, were charged tuition for private services, or were unable to obtain any type of services" (Wood 1992, p.9).

Public Law 94-142 also provided official sanction for the bureaucratic development of special education (Fisher and McGregor 1996). As a result of this law, many students with disabilities were placed in special education programs that were designed to accommodate the individual needs of the students. Much of the time students who were in special education programs were segregated from non-disabled students who were in the general education programs. Special education teachers designed curriculum and instruction based on the individual education plan (IEP) of the students in the classroom.

The Education for All Handicapped Children Act also stipulated that special education students should be provided their education in the "least restrictive environment." (More about least restrictive environment will follow in Chapter Three.)

In the mid-1970s, the consensus was that identified special education students should be a part of mainstream classes, when their special needs could be met in such an environment. Appropriate accommodations for the mainstreamed student in a general education class were to be designed so that the individualized education plan could be carried out in this setting. This was incorporated into the Education for All Handicapped Children Act of 1975 (Public Law 94-142), later known as the Individuals with Disabilities Education Act (IDEA). "IDEA also mandates that a continuum of alternative placements (CAP) be available to students with disabilities, under the assumption that an array of options ranging from full-time placements in general classrooms to placement in residential schools or hospitals is necessary to meet the needs of individual students. The IDEA further mandates that determination of appropriate services and placements be on an individual basis; it proscribes decisions based on categorizations of students" (Kauffman and Hallahan 1995, p.3; Choate 1997).

In 1997, changes were made in the legislation so that more students with disabilities could be serviced in general education programs when appropriate. "With the reauthorization of IDEA, June 4, 1997, Congress clearly spelled out the right of all children to fully participate and progress in the general curriculum. It also guaranteed the right of all children to benefit from a Free Appropriate Public Education (FAPE) with appropriate supports and services regardless of any disability. Another key premise is that all students have a right to a continuum of services to meet their individual needs" (Tilton 1997, p.14).

Individual states enacted specific laws that determined the delivery and implementation of special education services. Special education law in California requires that the IEP document specify the supplementary aids and services necessary to ensure a student's participation in the regular education program. [20 U.S.C. § 1414 (d)(1)(A)(iii)] Typical aids and services could include the following: special seating; test modifications to accommodate a student's disability; curriculum modifications; instructional, behavioral, or health aides when necessary; and adaptive equipment.

One of the significant changes in education is the manner in which students with disabilities are served. A major reason for this shift is what has become known as the "Regular Education Initiative" (REI). The regular education/special education initiative goes by many names — collaborative teaching, cooperative teaching, supported education, prereferral intervention, mainstream education, and, most commonly, the regular education initiative (REI) (Miller 1990; Robinson 1990). The REI calls for a restructuring of special and general education to create a partnership among educators from both disciplines to better serve all students (Wood 1992, p.28).

Supporters of the REI assert that the "two-box" system of general education and special education is dysfunctional and detrimental to students. Believing that most students can be taught in general education, advocates call for a merger of general and special education. Choate (1997) believes that this merger and the REI are supported conceptually by IDEA (p.3).

Choate explained, "Proponents of the REI claim that students, teachers, administrators, and parents will benefit from the merging of special education and general education wherein more students will participate in the mainstream of education. Advocates further assert that the REI will lead to minimizing the stigma of labels, increasing opportunity for modeling desired social and school survival behaviors, learning in situations that are more representative of the real world, and increasing appreciation and understanding of individual differences. While these consequences are positive, some educators question the benefits of REI. They argue that many special students will be lost in the shuffle, that general education teachers are ill-prepared to serve students with special needs, that there is no empirical basis for shifting to a full-inclusion model, and that research has yet to identify ways to effectively educate heterogeneous and diverse populations in large group settings, such as general education classrooms" (Choate 1997, pp. 14-15).

## Mainstreaming and Inclusion: What Is the Difference?

The terms *inclusion* and *mainstreaming* often are confused or used interchangeably. Adding to the confusion is the fact that mainstreaming is sometimes referred to as integration. It may be useful at this time to provide some operational definitions.

*Mainstreaming* refers to the practice of taking students with disabilities out of their separate self-contained classes and placing them in regular education classes, usually with no support services or instructional modification and with the expectations that they function on the same level as their non-disabled peers in the regular educational classroom. Students are usually considered "visitors" (Dipalma 1995, p.1). "The placement in the regular classroom for a certain number of these students [identified special education students] will depend on what subjects are best presented in such a setting. The doors of the regular [general education] and special education classrooms must be kept open so that special students can move freely back and forth between them" (Joynt and Blackwell 1980, p.2).

The educator most responsible for the mainstreamed special education students' program is the special educator. "Mainstreaming does not mean that the special education teacher/or resource personnel trained to work with such students turn over their responsibilities to the regular teacher" (Joynt and Blackwell 1980, p.2).

*Inclusion* refers to the practice of placing students with disabilities in the general classroom with the necessary supports and services to enable them to participate in a general education class. "Expectations are based on the student's individual needs and goals, not necessarily the same grade level as the other students in the class. Students with disabilities are not considered 'visitors,' but are an integral part of a class and school community" (Dipalma 1995, p.1).

In other words, a special education student who is mainstreamed usually does not have additional adult support in the general education class. Additionally, curriculum and instruction would not be modified for the mainstreamed student. The special education student who is included often does have additional adult support (i.e., a one-to-one educational assistant and consultant special education teacher). Curriculum and instruction are almost always modified.

Inclusion advocates recognize the need for specific services for individual special education. These services could include speech therapy, occupational therapy, physical therapy and other services. Services such as these have traditionally been provided outside of the classroom and have been referred to as "pull-out" services. Inclusion advocates prefer these services be delivered as a "push-in" service. In this manner the speech therapist, or other educators providing specialized instruction, would deliver the services within the general education classroom. Obviously, appropriate modifications would have to be made in the general education classroom. "Advocates for inclusion support the need for specialized services, but do not support separate education. Advocates are concerned about the lower expectations educators frequently have for students in special education, as well as the social isolation that results from students going to classes and schools with students who are not from their community" (Fisher and McGregor 1996, pp. 1&2).

According to Stainback and Stainback (1994), full inclusion is the education of all students in neighborhood classrooms and schools. "Inclusion is a term that is frequently used to describe the right of all students to shared access to the general curriculum. Another name may be Heterogeneous Education. The name itself is only a beginning. Inclusion is so much more than physical placement of a student with special needs in the general classroom. It really involves a system-wide change and a philosophy in which every student is accepted, every student belongs and is a valued member of the learning community" (Tilton 1997, p.14).

There are those who advocate for full inclusion for all students. "Full inclusion refers to the provision of appropriate educational services to all students in regular classes attended by nondisabled students of the same chronological age in their neighborhood school, including students with severe disabilities" (Giangreco and Putnam 1991, p.245). This does not take into consideration a case-by-case study of each individual student and that student's needs. The least restrictive environment continuum then is overridden because full inclusion advocates believe the benefits are immense. "It should be stressed that the major reason for full inclusion is not that previously excluded students are necessarily going to become proficient in socialization, history, or math facts, although it is obvious that there are more opportunities for everyone to grow and learn in integrated classrooms, rather, inclusion of all students teaches the student and his or her peers that all people are equally valued members of this society, and that it is worthwhile to include everyone. The previously accepted mode of dealing with differences among people was segregation, which communicates the message that either we do not want to accept everyone or that some people are not worth the effort to make the necessary accommodations to include them" (Stainback, Stainback and Moravec 1994, p.82).

It is a common complaint of many teachers that full inclusion will have a negative impact on the other students in the class. This is particularly true if the student's disability causes serious behavior problems. Disagreements between advocates of full inclusion and others, who believe a case-by-case decision for inclusion should be made, has caused contention.

## The Surrounding Controversy

When the inclusion movement started taking hold in schools throughout the country there was much derision, which continues today. Educators and parents have strong feelings and disagreements about how students with disabilities should be educated and in what setting. "Faced with the pressures of mainstreaming and inclusion, general and special educators, administrators, and parents have engaged in widespread and sometimes contentious debate" (Choate 1997, p.15).

In order for inclusion to be successful a significant amount of groundwork must be done and many supports must be in place. "Students with special needs challenge a teacher's ability to individualize instruction, support positive relationships among students, and collaborate with parents. Thus they challenge the principal's ability to lead positive change and support teachers and specialists staff as they expand their competence" (O'Brien and Forrest 1989, p.2). A lack of preparation causes a great deal of pressure on educators, leaving them feeling powerless and angry. Additionally, many teachers feel that decisions about including students are not based on the individual needs of the student, but rather are based on financial concern and/or convenience.

Teachers also are upset by what they see as inappropriate parental pressure. Some teachers feel that parents make decisions that they are not qualified to make. Parents, however, feel that they know their child better than anyone else does and often feel they are being "kept out of the loop."

Teachers in inclusionary situations often feel overwhelmed by having to work with too many students with special needs. "For many of these teachers, accommodating the students' academic and behavioral difficulties requires considerable effort or may even necessitate instructional expertise they have not yet acquired" (Heckman and Rike 1994, p.30). The American Federation of Teachers has publicly stated their opposition to full inclusion, saying teachers aren't adequately trained to deal with the wide range of disabilities, physical and emotional (Feldman 1994).

Additionally, teachers worry that having a student with disabilities in their class will disadvantage other students in that class. They also worry that the parents of non-disabled students will have a negative reaction to their children being in classes with students who are disabled. This is particularly true when students with disabilities have behavioral problems.

In 1994, Albert Shanker, President of the American Federation of Teachers stated his disapproval of the placement of all students with disabilities in regular education classrooms without regard to the nature or severity of the student's disability, the student's ability to function in the class, the educational benefits, or the impact on the rest of the class. Shanker said he was in favor of inclusion is some cases. "I do believe very large numbers of students now separated into special education could be included and integrated into regular classes and it would be beneficial." He warned against inclusion decisions that were not based on student needs. "Full inclusion is becoming more widely practiced based on budgetary and social motivation and not what most Americans think classrooms ought to be about, which is education."

One essential difficulty of the full inclusion philosophy is that it presumes that children with learning disabilities or with developmental disabilities would be studying the same curriculum as the average student — just, perhaps, at a slower pace (Will 1984). "In reality, at the middle school or junior high school level, many specialists in the field of mental retardation stress a functional curriculum with concrete tasks and usable skills, such as computing sales tax, reading job descriptions, or writing a menu for a balanced diet. Many specialists recommend a curriculum for such students that focuses on learning useful skills and understandings that do not require a heavy burden of generalization or transfer. Such a functional curriculum is not the preferred intellectual meal, however, for above-average students on their way to college. Nor is the abstract generalization required by the curriculum in college preparatory classes the proper educational diet for children with mental retardation" (Gallagher 1995, p.99).

Other pressures of teaching confound the pressure of dealing with identified special education students. "What has changed in most schools is that today's teachers and schools are under tremendous pressure regarding achievement on paper-and-pencil assessments. In state after state, assessments are being used to measure pupils' progress. Results are reported by the mass media and used as measuring sticks, not for individual students, but for teachers, principals and schools. Research on schools with such high-stakes testing, plus the pressures of dealing with today's angry, violent children, makes teaching an extremely stressful profession and having to deal with students with disabilities in the classroom will not make it any easier" (Carr 1995, p.266).

Full inclusion could have a deleterious effect on some students who are inappropriately included. "I predict that if inclusion becomes a reality, the dropout rate for students with LD will soar to a nationally disgraceful figure. I predict that the number of teenagers turning to drugs or alcohol will soar. I predict that an epidemic of teenage suicides will wrap families in despair and grief" (Carr 1995, p.266).

Advocates of inclusion give compelling examples of numerous benefits to both special education students and non-identified students. Hardman, McDonnell and McDonnell (1989), expressed concerns about what happens when the network of family and friends is not established or is disrupted by placement beyond the boundaries of the neighborhood community. They believe family involvement is compromised and school programs are less likely to reflect curricular content relevant to the community where the student lives and spends his or her nonschool time. Additional concerns include the possibility of limited access to extracurricular activities and that other members of the community do not experience the necessary opportunities to develop both the social commitment and skills needed to include individuals who require varying levels of support.

Specific advantages of inclusion programs for students with disabilities include, opportunities to model age-appropriate social behavior, opportunities to develop adaptive behavior in a normalized environment, exposure

**17**

to age-appropriate information and related vocabulary, opportunities to model on-task behavior, and to participate in normalized school activities and greater social opportunities in the community.

There are, however, possible disadvantages associated with inclusion. One disadvantage is the possibility that disabled students could end up feeling isolated because other students prefer to socialize with students who already demonstrate appropriate social behavior. Disabled students also can feel overwhelmed by the environmental demands of a normalized environment. Additionally, "disabled students can feel left out because they do not understand what is being discussed, or feel frustrated because normalized activities may be too challenging" (Dipalma 1995, pp.6&7).

An increase in behavior problems is always a concern for teachers. For those who argue that inclusion adds too much teacher stress because of an increase in behavior problems, advocates answer that there will always be this type of stress. "Inclusion is one factor that contributes to teacher stress. However, even without inclusion, every school has several students who stand out because of their behavior" (Vandover 1996, p.1).

Dipalma (1995) documented possible benefits of inclusion for educational professionals and other educational staff that include gaining a shared knowledge of instructional strategies and best practices from both general education and special education faculty, and the provision of transdisciplinary training and peer coaching to enhance and improve educational experiences for all children. Inclusion also increases the number and type of roles both general and special education teachers can pursue on a career ladder without having to leave teaching (p.5).

Richard Villa, in *Creating an Inclusive School*, discussed when inclusion has been successful. Inclusion, he says, has been most successful where it has been part of a broad general reform of general education. In many schools, the presence of children with disabilities has sparked other reform initiatives, such as team teaching, peer teaching, cooperative learning, authentic assessment, and thematic interdisciplinary instruction (1995). Students have a right to be educated with students who are not disabled. This right is overruled only when supplementary aids and services cannot achieve a satisfactory education.

Some of the indicators of successful inclusive education are, "positive community attitude, commitment of staff, parental understanding, preparation, feeling of control, adequate resources and administrative support" (Dipalma 1995, p.24).

Clare Royal was a special education teacher for 17 years. She served as a special education coordinator for three years. Currently she is an elementary school principal. She discussed the benefits of including students with disabilities into regular education programs.

*When you include students with special needs into regular education programs, the*

> *children, as well as the professionals, are*
> *exposed to the fact that students don't come*
> *in "one size fits all." Students begin to accept*
> *others who are different. They also begin to*
> *see that although these students may have*
> *labels, or special equipment or different ways*
> *they behave, they are more like themselves*
> *than different. I think it's a win-win situation*
> *for both groups of kids. They learn from each*
> *other. They realize that there are a lot of peo-*
> *ple who make up this world.*

Royal acknowledges that having students with disabilities can add an extra burden to the regular education teacher.

> *I think the difficulty is that in this day and age*
> *when we are trying to "raise the bar" to raise*
> *standards, and try to do more with less, (teach-*
> *ers have larger class sizes, the curriculum is*
> *more intense), time seems to be a problem for*
> *teachers. They want to do the right thing for all*
> *kids, but they feel there is not enough time to*
> *collaborate and to do the job fully. In many*
> *ways teachers feel overwhelmed.*

Royal spoke about how teachers can be supported.

> *Schools need to do their homework. By this*
> *I mean the building administrator, the*
> *social worker, the psychologist, and the*
> *ancillary staff really need to have some*
> *pre-requisite knowledge of the child with*

*special needs. We can do some groundwork with and for the teacher. We can start the wheel turning to develop a good behavior plan. We can do training for the teacher. My role is to be a sounding board for the teachers. I need to be a good listener. We need to reach out of our four walls and hook up with other professionals. I share research articles. I share tips from other teachers. I share ideas from my own classroom experience. I give teachers release time to look at other classes and other programs. I sometimes go in and model teaching methods.*

By providing extra support for teachers dealing with students with disabilities in their classrooms, particularly those students who have behavioral problems, the added burden can be relieved.

**21**

# Chapter Three

# Least Restrictive Environment

The Individuals with Disabilities Education Act (IDEA) defines least restrictive environment in this manner:

> that to the maximum extent appropriate, handicapped children are educated with children who are not handicapped; and removal from the regular educational environment occurs only when the nature or severity of the handicap is such that education in regular classes with the use of supplementary aids and services cannot be achieved satisfactorily.

The legislation further stipulates that —

> The nature of the student's disability and individual needs could make it appropriate for the student to be placed in a setting outside of the regular educational environment in order to ensure that the student's IEP [individual education plan] is satisfactorily implemented.

Most legislation is subject to interpretation. Individuals who advocate one way or another will always

**23**

interpret legislation to benefit their cause. As with inclusionary practices, there are disagreements as to what least restrictive environment means in a practical sense. Inclusion advocates interpret the legislation to mean that under almost all circumstances students with special needs should be educated in the general education population. "The Least Restrictive Environment (LRE) is the method of providing maximum feasible integration with peers. Generally this means placing most students in the general classroom as much as possible" (Tilton 1997, p.15). As students in restrictive classroom environments progress, they should be placed in less restrictive environments. "In implementing the continuum of services model and in concert with the goals of IDEA, the aim of instruction is to advance students as quickly as possible through the mastery of knowledge and skills which will allow them to move into less restrictive placements" (Choate 1997, p.10). In other words, even when a student with a disability is in a more restrictive or more segregated program one of the educational goals should be to increase the skills of that student to, in part, enable him or her to move into a less restrictive environment.

There are stipulations in the law that allow classroom placements that are more restrictive. These classroom placements may include programs housed outside of the home school and outside of the home school district for those students who cannot be accommodated or adequately educated in lesser restrictive environments. "The law does provide for a continuum of services recognizing that, for a small number of students, a setting other than the general classroom may be appropriate. The burden of proof in placing students with disabilities in a setting other than the general classroom lies with the school district" (Tilton 1997, p.197).

In 1995, Assistant Secretary Judith Heumann from the Office of Special Education and Rehabilitative Services, and Director Thomas Hehir from the Office of Special Education Programs addressed the placement issue of least restrictive environment: "Recognizing that the regular classroom may not be the LRE placement for every disabled student, the Part B regulations require public agencies to make available a continuum of alternative placement, or a range of placement options, to meet the needs of students with disabilities for special education and related services." Particular emphasis was placed on the fact that Part B requires that a student's placement must be based on the individual education plan (IEP) of the disabled student. Additionally, placements cannot be based solely on factors such as category of disability, severity of disability, configuration of delivery system, availability of education or related services, availability of space, or convenience to administration. In other words, a school district cannot deny a student a least restrictive environment placement based on the fact that the school district does not have the appropriate program housed in the student's home school or in the home district.

The placement of an individual student with a disability in the least restrictive environment must take into account the following factors:

- Provision of the special education services needed by the student.

- Provision for education of the student to the maximum extent appropriate to the needs of the student with other students who do not have disabilities.

- Provision of a placement that is as close as possible to the student's home school.

Kauffman and Hallahan (1995) feel that inclusion advocates believe that "all individual consideration was to be constrained by universal placement of students with disabilities in general schools and classes" (p.3). They further imply that this violates the spirit of the least restrictive environment by ignoring the continuum of services. The law states, "In other words there is an assumption that any single placement is not appropriate for meeting the diverse needs of all students with disabilities" (Kauffman and Hallahan 1995, p.6). "The service delivery model proposed for full inclusion therefore is one in which students are not removed from general education classes, and all services are brought to them in that setting" (Kauffman and Hallahan 1995, p.7). In essence, the argument of full inclusion advocates is that students with disabilities no longer be included in a general classroom when, and to the extent appropriate, based on case-by-case evaluation; rather, they argued, students with disabilities should be treated, for purposes of placement, as a single category or class. Kauffman and Hallahan (1995) feel that advocates of full inclusion believe that all students should, at all times, be educated in a general education program no matter what the disability is, and no matter what services the student with disabilities needs.

Some educators are deeply concerned about the removal of other placement options and the consequence of such removal. "If you eliminate the continuum that includes a resource room you limit the options for placement, thus a student with disabilities who could use the support of a resource room may have only a self-contained classroom as an option" (Kauffman and Hallahan 1995). Obviously, placing a student with mild disabilities in a self-contained program would not be beneficial to that student and would clearly violate the tenets of least restrictive environment. The question is — Will every student be appropriate for a full inclusion program?

Kauffman and Hallahan (1995) concede that some students now being served primarily in resource rooms or special education classes could be spending more of their time in general education classes. They also state, however, that "to propose that all students with disabilities can be educated all of the time in general education classrooms defies logic" (p.9).

The key to the successful placement of a student with disabilities is to review each case on an individual basis. Placement in LRE requires an individual decision, based on each child's IEP, and based on the strong presumption of the idea that children with disabilities be educated in general education classes with appropriate aids and supports. (64 Fed. Reg. 12637 (1999)) Placement should be determined after all the educational needs of the individual

**27**

student have been established. Therefore, decisions about placement should only occur after the IEP is written. Placement decisions, including level and location of intervention and regrouping of students, are reviewed at least once a year, or more frequently, if requested by a member of the IEP team. The Pennsylvania Department of Education outlined inappropriate placement decisions. "Placements outside the regular school must be considered solely on the basis of the student's needs. Students are not to be placed in separate facilities because of low pupil to teacher ratios, availability of services, availability of space in regular buildings, because certain categories of disability such as autism or seriously emotionally disturbed are unavailable in regular education or because sufficient staff or receptive regular education teachers and administrators are not available."

Determining the proper placement for a student, whether it is in a fully included program or a more restrictive environment, is by no means an easy task. It is often difficult to predict how any individual student will do in any individual classroom environment. "The accumulated research offers no definitive answers regarding the most appropriate placement option(s) for students with disabilities. Several decades of so-called efficacy studies have failed to produce a clear-cut picture of the most appropriate educational alternatives" (Choate 1997, p.13).

A major concern of many educators is the frequency and intensity of distracting, disruptive, and dangerous behavior that some included students with disabilities bring with them into a general education program. The impact of their behavior on the other students in the class, and the teacher's ability to teach the required curriculum, is often discussed in the faculty room. The determination of appropriate placement for a child whose behavior is interfering with the education of others, requires careful consideration as to whether the child can appropriately function well enough in the general education classroom, if provided the proper behavioral supports, strategies and interventions. If the child can appropriately function in such an educational setting with supports, placement in a more restrictive environment would be inconsistent with the least restrictive environment provisions of the IDEA. (64 Fed. Reg. 12637 (1999)) Unfortunately, it is difficult to predict the behavior of students in different educational settings. There are many factors that are involved. These factors include, but are not limited to, the teaching style of the teachers, the composition of the student population in the class and school, the willingness of staff to work with the student with disabilities, and the level of comfort the student who is disabled has in that environment.

Naturally, a disabled child can be placed outside of the regular educational environment. However, the full range of supplementary aids and services that, if provided, would facilitate the student's placement in the general classroom setting, must be considered. (34 C.F.R. Part 300, Appendix A, Question 1; 64 Fed. Reg. 12471 (1999))

Sometimes, particularly with students who have significant behavior problems, a change in school or district gives that student a chance for a "new start" and can help remove that student from negative influences encountered at the local school. A bad reputation in one school can turn into a positive reputation in another setting. Of course, all appropriate modifications specified in that student's individualized educational program needs to be in place, regardless of where the student is being educated. This may include the disabled student receiving an educational program in general education classes, even though they may not be in the student's home school or home district.

Once the placement decision has been made, and the student is placed in the least restrictive environment, the educator's job is just beginning. "The insurance that the special education student receives the best alternative educational consideration possible must be closely monitored. His physical presence in a regular class does not guarantee that he will receive an appropriate educational learning experience, nor is it guaranteed in the special class. What needs to be guaranteed, however, is that in either setting the special education student is provided with the opportunity for an appropriate educational learning experience. Careful monitoring of the learning experience is necessary by all teachers involved" (Joynt and Blackwell 1980, p.2). A lack of preparation and implementation of the disabled student's program is where most inclusion programs fail. This will be discussed in later chapters of the book.

It cannot be stressed enough that educators need to be prepared to meet the challenges and demands of accommodating students in the least restrictive environment. "The steady movement of students with disabilities into less restrictive settings requires general educators to teach a significantly more diverse classroom population" (Choate 1997, p.3). Training and support for educators to meet the demand and challenges are essential for success.

Elizabeth Northland is an attorney who concentrates her practice in public education, particularly special education law. Northland's work with children with disabilities began in the early 1970s when, as a social worker with the State Office of Mental Retardation and Developmental Disabilities, she worked to bring institutionalized adults with disabilities back to our communities and advocated on behalf of young children with disabilities and their families to secure appropriate services through the public schools. After several years of advocating on behalf of people with disabilities, in the late 1970s Ms. Northland went back to school to become a lawyer. Following law school, she resumed her work on behalf of children. As a person interested in addressing systemic barriers, she joined the state education department where she worked for six years and where she remained through the mid-1990s. As someone who had been integrally involved in the implementation of a federal law, which held out a promise that children with disabilities were entitled to receive a free appropriate public education in the least restrictive environment, she reflected on both the legislative intent and the implementation and evolution of the federal law:

> *The promise of a free appropriate public education affords children with disabilities the right to meaningful educational oppor-tunities and genuine access to public edu-*

**31**

*cation. Congress never intended to offer students with disabilities the opportunity to maximize educational benefits. Instead its goal was to ensure that the doors of public school education were open to children with disabilities. However, if state or federal law provided children who were not disabled with educational opportunities designed to maximize each student's potential, it would be discriminatory to offer a child with a disability anything less.*

Ms. Northland spoke about the challenges facing both public schools and parents in providing services to children with disabilities in the least restrictive environment:

*The prevailing thought in the implementation of the law in 1975 was to protect children with disabilities from the pressures of regular education. In order to protect them, our state placed an emphasis on small classes designed to meet the needs of children with disabilities, with a separate and less challenging curriculum, where they could feel successful. The federal law, from its inception, only authorized the removal of children with disabilities from the regular educational environment, when, due to the nature or severity of the child's disability, that education in regular classes with the use of supplementary aids and services could not be achieved satisfactorily. (20 U.S.C. § 1412(a)(5)) In 1997, Congress reinforced its original commitment to educating children with disabilities in regular classrooms when it added a provision that requires school districts to explain the extent, if any, to which the child will not participate with non-disabled children in regular classes. (20 U.S.C. § 1414(d)(1)(A)(iv)) In effect, this provision created a "rebuttable presumption" that all children with disabilities are entitled to full participation in regular classes, except where such placement would deprive them of an appropriate education.*

Ms. Northland further explained the difficulty of determining what an appropriate education is and what the least restrictive environment is for individual students:

*There is no fixed definition of what constitutes an "appropriate education" and no two cases are the same. This is not a science, and there is no formula. To the extent IEP teams must develop and review an individualized educational program at least once a year based on the individual needs of the child, with annual goals and objectives designed to meet those needs, and a program of special education, supplementary aids and services offered in the least restrictive environment appropriate to enable the child to benefit from the curric-*

> *ulum and reach the student's goals, that is the closest we come to a prescribed formula for defining an appropriate educational program. Apart from that, an appropriate program is one that works — we know it when we see it . . . the child is responding well to the environment and is able to meet his or her goals. The child is able to remain on task, the academics are presented in a way that is challenging at the same time it is understandable . . . and the child's stress level is manageable.*

Ms. Northland believes there is merit to drafting the IEP before placement decisions are made:

> *Given the complexities of a well-written IEP, having a draft prepared by the people who know the child best makes the most sense. If parents and district personnel take the time to work together to develop that draft, almost always, we can reach consensus on a child's needs and the goals of the special educational program. To the extent there is controversy, it usually comes down to the manner in which the program will be delivered . . . it is too restrictive . . . not restrictive enough? What services does the child need at what level of intensity? Testing accommodations? . . . curriculum modifications etc., etc., etc. The answers, however, revert back to the description of needs and the goals and*

*objectives set for the child. Once we have consensus in those areas, with good baseline information, current evaluations, and a solid understanding of the general curriculum, the discussion about placement and program should flow. That discussion is the culmination . . . a natural outgrowth of the students needs and goals.*

Sometimes the pressure to provide what the educators/and or parents see as the least restrictive environment causes serious problems:

*One of the problems we come up against, is when district personnel or parents see the principle of least restrictive environment and a child's right to be educated in the regular education setting as an absolute. Placement in a regular education setting is not always "best," it is not always "appropriate," and sometimes it can become very destructive for the disabled students, the other students and the classroom as a whole.*

When placement is not correct, Northland explained, it's the children who suffer.

*There are children whose behaviors become the only way they can express to the adults in their world just how upset they are. They will act out their feelings in the classroom in front of their peers. While they are desperately trying to tell us something, we are*

*looking for experts, offering intensive train-
ing, looking for the quick fix, when there are
many instances where it doesn't exist. Then
the question becomes, how long do we continue to maintain the child in a situation that
is clearly not working nor (is) in the child's
best interest, if even for the time being?
How long does the parent, in frustration,
blame the staff for not knowing how to
address the child's disabilities, and when do
we begin to look at the environment itself
and ask whether it can or should be con-
verted into one that does? Or, the other
extreme, how long does the district wait,
before it recognizes the fact that the child is
falling further and further behind in regular
education? In other words, do we let the student fail before we offer a more structured
setting? Sometimes it's the proverbial
square peg in the round hole. There is a reason programs don't work for kids . . . the
reason is often that the environment simply
isn't designed to meet the needs of the child.
At some point, the answer lies in a change in
the environment where we can help the child
to develop the skills that may enable him or
her to function successfully in less-struc-
tured settings — as opposed to adjusting an
environment that is not fundamentally and
essentially designed to meet the needs of the
child. It takes a flexible approach . . . one*

*that is constantly responsive to the changing needs of the child.*

The school itself may be another obstacle that causes district problems when trying to provide educational opportunities for children with disabilities in the least restrictive environment. Ms. Northland adds:

*Another problem is the physical plant — the design of the school building itself. Every time I go into a new school I want to see how the classrooms are configured to see whether the physical plant is set up to accommodate children with special needs. I think we need different classroom configurations and a lot of flexibility . . . learning centers . . . rooms that allow students to regain their composure, etc. Until we build schools to accommodate children with special needs it will be difficult for school districts to offer a genuine continuum of services within our public schools. We need architects and educators working together to develop blue prints that design school buildings for full inclusion. Oh, and another thought, who devised smaller classrooms only for children with disabilities? Many students require smaller classes to benefit educationally . . . this is not a need reserved for children with disabilities. Many students need individualized instruction geared toward their style of learning.*

*Once we provide smaller classes to any student who requires them, we can offer smaller classrooms for children who need them, without regard to whether they are labeled as a person with a disability. That would probably eliminate the majority of our separate classrooms. Perhaps, that is where we need to focus our energies. With full federal funding for special education . . . perhaps we could improve opportunities for all students . . . and who knows . . . for those children who require smaller classrooms to benefit . . . perhaps we will see an unanticipated benefit . . . a reduction in the number of students we need to identify as children with disabilities.*

## Features of a Least Restrictive Environment

## Summary

Least restrictive environment legislation hopes to ensure that, whenever possible, students with disabilities are taught in the same school they would attend if they were not disabled. Decisions concerning a student's educational program are based on that particular student's needs. Each student is educated in the least restrictive environment appropriate to the individual student. The placement decision is made after developing the goals and objectives of the student's IEP. Based on the needed education and related services, the parents and school decide where the student is to be placed. Placement decisions are reviewed at least once a year to ensure that the program is meeting the student's needs.

Whenever possible students with disabilities are taught in general education classes with their non-disabled peers. To facilitate the efforts of the student and the educational staff, provisions and accommodations must be built into the program. The student, the classroom teacher, and other educational staff should be provided the supports needed to make the placement successful. Special services such as speech therapy, physical therapy, etc., are provided in the school and, when possible, in the actual general education class. Students who cannot be fully integrated into general education classes are integrated to the greatest extent possible. Whatever the placement, positive attitudes and social integration should be actively promoted. School personnel should receive supportive training. Students with disabilities should receive the necessary and appropriate support and training that will facilitate an education that will enable them to live as complete a life as possible. Junior high school students should be provided with career planning, counseling services, and pre-vocational skill training. Secondary school students should be provided opportunities to learn practical vocational and community living skills at normal community training sites.

Educational staff should receive training and assistance from administrators to ensure a sound educational program for the student with special needs, as well as for the other students in the classroom.

# Chapter Four

# Groundwork for Successful Mainstreaming and Inclusionary Programs

## Mainstreaming

When a mainstreaming program has been recommended and agreed upon by the IEP team, careful preparation must take place. The students must be prepared for the classroom environment, and the classroom environment must be prepared for the students.

It can be frightening for a student with disabilities who is transferring from a self-contained program into a new program that offers fewer supports. The student may feel anxious about expectations of having greater responsibilities. These students often worry about whether they will fit in with their peers and may suffer from a "fear of failing."

There also may be a sense of pride and excitement when a student from a self-contained program is beginning a mainstreaming program. In addition, some students are delighted to be in mainstreamed situations where there are more opportunities for social interaction. Additionally, some of these students welcome the

**41**

possibility of a more challenging academic program. If the student succeeds in overcoming the challenges of a more difficult curriculum, the sense of self-satisfaction can be wonderful.

However, a newly identified student who is coming from a total inclusionary program into a mainstreaming program may feel a sense of loss. The student may feel as if he failed or was a let down to others. Students in this situation also may feel that they will lose their friends or that others will make fun of them. On the other hand, it is possible that the student will be coming from a situation that was difficult and frustrating. Sometimes these students feel a sense of relief because they will be more protected and may have expectations of greater success.

Additional assistance with instruction and curriculum, and appropriate modifications may be needed for a temporary period. Often a student with special needs has specific deficits in skill areas. Assistance can "catch the student up" and facilitate a full return to the inclusionary and/or general education program.

Preparing the identified student is as important for the student as it is for the educational staff that will be working with him or her. An introduction to all educational staff with whom the student will be working, and visits prior to the switch, are usually beneficial in allaying the anxieties of the student, as well as the educational staff members. "Gradual entrance of the special education students into the regular classroom must be cautiously handled" (Joynt and Blackwell 1980, pp.2-3). Sensitivity to the following points must be considered.

(a) The impact upon both the general and special education students in the area of acceptance.

(b) The cooperation of the general educator to willingly accept these special students.

(c) The cooperation of the resource personnel and special education student to assist the general classroom teacher.

(d) The flexibility exhibited by both general education and special education classroom teachers so that the students can move easily within different educational settings.

The crucial factor in a mainstreaming program is how the needs of the identified students should be met. "There are three key educational objectives that should be considered in helping to meet the needs of the mainstreamed special education student: first, appropriate individualized assessment; second, the utilization of key resource personnel; third, the development and utilization of individualized program plans. All three of these educational objectives must be closely considered by the professional staff in charge" (Joynt and Blackwell 1980, p.6). Having plans about what will happen and when it will happen organizes the program and helps guarantee that the student is receiving the supports he or she needs. It also helps the educational staff members, who usually feel more comfortable when they know exactly what their roles and tasks are. All educational staff members, parents, and the student should be included in developing an appropriate plan.

**43**

General education and special education teachers need to combine their areas of expertise to develop and implement an appropriate program for the student with special needs. "To ensure the success of students in the mainstream, educators must establish an alliance that combines general educators' knowledge of what to teach with special educators' knowledge of how to teach. By pooling these two bodies of information, many school districts should succeed in mainstreaming students with disabilities" (Choate 1997, p.16).

There is no doubt that the preparation needed to successfully mainstream a student can be burdensome to the educational team involved. "The current trend toward the placement of students with disabilities into general education places ever-increasing responsibility on the general educator to design individualized education programs for these students. Much of the responsibility for successfully mainstreaming students with disabilities rests with the multidisciplinary team, including the general education teacher" (Choate 1997, p.16). It is important that the team is supported by administration.

Perhaps the time has come to train both general and special educators in the same way. Additionally, it is vital to train both general educators and special educators to have knowledge of what and how to teach. Many authorities believe that it is possible and desirable to bridge the gap between general and special education and to merge the knowledge and expertise of these two professional disciplines. Educational administrators also require training and need to take the lead in showing acceptance of students with disabilities. Administrators who have a positive attitude and provide the necessary training for educational staff will have schools and programs that successfully work with students with disabilities. If the educational staff do not feel that they have the proper training to work with students with disabilities, the classroom program and the students suffer. "Survey studies indicate that general classroom teachers who express negative views toward mainstreaming often feel ill prepared and unsupported in that effort" (Choate 1997, p.16).

Robin Wayne is a veteran elementary school teacher who usually has a class size of 25 to 30 students. Ms. Wayne, from year to year, would receive mainstreamed students from the self-contained special education classroom housed in the school where she taught. Jessica Handleman, a new teacher, was one of the special education teachers for those mainstreamed students. The two worked closely and met daily to discuss the progress of mainstreamed students.

Ms. Handleman discussed why she chose to mainstream students into Ms. Wayne's class:

> *I checked out Robin's class. Robin was a wonderful teacher. She was patient and creative. Many of the designed activities were "hands-on" types of activities. The most wonderful thing about Robin, as a teacher, was that she taught her students tolerance for others. I felt that my students would do quite well in her classroom. When I approached Robin about main-streaming two of my students into her*

*classroom she was very receptive. I had a sense that my students would feel safe, comfortable, and happy in her classroom.*

And the students experienced few problems, Ms. Wayne said.

*When the students from Jessica's class first arrived, they were very quiet. They were observers who watched everything. My classroom was a busy place with lots of activities going on. With time they became more a part of the group. For the most part, academically, they didn't do anything less than my students did, but they didn't do anything more. There were very few behavior problems. When there were, Jessica and I talked it over.*

What were the benefits of mainstreaming? Ms. Handleman saw the following:

*The students who were mainstreamed into Robin's class loved going there. This encouraged other students in my class to venture out as well. I felt confident that my students were receiving what they needed both academically and socially. I also think that working with Robin, a veteran teacher, helped me as a new teacher. Robin was supportive and always willing to help me in anyway she could. I asked her for advice often. I still use many of the tips she gave me.*

Ms. Wayne also saw the benefits.

*I informed my class that two students would be coming into the class. I asked them how they could welcome those students and make them feel comfortable. I know that kids don't do well when they don't feel comfortable. I had some students who were somewhat asocial. They didn't seem to reach out to others. After the students from Jessica's class arrived, I saw them, after a while, reaching out to them. It was as if they were under some peer pressure to do that because we had talked about it, and they saw their classmates doing it. I also think that all of my students gained a better understanding that "different" kids are not really different. I remember a time when one of Jessica's students wrote a story that was quite lively. I had him read it out loud to the class. My students listened carefully. They were curious about what this kid could do. I think they were impressed with him.*

But there were disadvantages to mainstreaming, too. Ms. Wayne said:

*Well, for one thing, it means that everyone else gets a little less attention. I had a large number of students, and adding a few more, meant I had less time to spend with each one. I also had to plan for, read, and evaluate the work of the mainstreamed students.*

Ms. Wayne, in conclusion, reported that mainstreaming students into her program was a positive experience. She was glad she did it and continued to accept mainstreamed students into her classroom.

*I learned something about myself that, at least in that instance, being flexible paid off. Getting to know those kids was beneficial for me too.*

A few years later Ms. Handleman transferred to one of the middle schools in the district and continued to mainstream students into general education classes. But this was a bit more difficult.

*It was a bit trickier mainstreaming students at the middle school level. For one thing, there were many more teachers and classes to keep track of. I had to be more organized about keeping track of the students . . . their assignments, homework, and classroom behavior. Eventually, I developed a chart, which helped me keep track of what was going on. It was hard at times. I tried not to impose on the general education teachers, but at the same time I needed to know how my students were doing. Most of the general education teachers were fine about talking and meeting with me. There were, however, some who made it very clear that they were not going to spend time after or before school discussing my students. I had to be creative about when and how to meet with those teachers.*

From Ms. Handleman's perspective the keys to successful mainstreaming are:

*I think one of the biggest keys is "the fit" between the individual student and teacher. I was very selective about who was going to what class with a specific teacher. I would not mainstream one of my students into the class of a teacher who, I could sense, was not comfortable accepting my students. Most of my students were classified "emotionally disturbed." There was too much at risk, if the mainstreaming experience was negative because of friction between the student and the teacher. Before mainstreaming a student, I would make sure that the curriculum and instructional style of the class and the teacher would be one that my student could handle, or at least handle with my assistance and modifications.*

Keeping the mainstreaming experience positive requires ongoing evaluation and follow-through:

**49**

*I kept up with all the teachers who had students of mine mainstreamed into my class. This was not an easy task. I spent many long hours at work, but I felt it was worth it. I did this to not only support the student, but to support the teachers as well. I knew that mainstreaming my students into their classes created an extra burden for them as well. I really tried to stay on top of it. It was very important for my students to know that I was following what was going on. I tried to make them think I knew about everything that went on in their mainstreamed classes. Of course, this was impossible, but if my students believed it, it kept them on their toes.*

Not all students who were mainstreamed were successful according to Handleman —

*There were some kids who just <u>couldn't</u> handle the mainstreaming situation or just <u>didn't want to</u> handle the mainstreaming situation. There were students who just refused to do any of the work and some who would act out so that they would be thrown out of the class. I even had a few who refused to leave my classroom. I think for these kids it was just too emotionally hard for them. They felt successful and protected in my room. They knew nobody would make fun of them, and they also* *knew that I wouldn't let the academic work become too frustrating. I would like to say that most of my students wanted to be mainstreamed and those students did pretty well. Sometimes a particular student just needs more time. I remember one student, Bobby. He had a terrific year with me. He was in seventh-grade. School had been a nightmare for him before that. Well . . . the powers that be decided that since he had done so well they were going to put him back in a totally included program. Bobby was horrified. His parents and I advocated for one more year in my program, but it just didn't happen. The next year he went back to a fully included program at his home middle school. After several weeks he became so distraught that he refused to go back to school. When he was forced to he brought a knife with him. I'm not sure if he was trying to protect himself or just get himself kicked out of the school. The poor kid ended up in a residential placement. I still feel so badly about that. Of course that was an extreme case. I wonder where he is today and how he's doing.*

Ms. Handleman helped the students in the general education classes accept the students from her program.

*I realized that if I didn't get involved with the school culture I wouldn't know how best to help my students. I became very active in the middle school. I worked in the after-school program, I chaperoned dances, I went to sporting events and I always went on the three-day eighth-grade class trip. I would often tell the students in my class what went on during these activities. Some of my students became curious and started to come to some of the activities. Others felt safe if they knew I was going to be there. I remember a mother came up to me after her daughter attended a school dance. She just about had tears in her eyes when she told me how happy she was that her daughter went to the dance. Her daughter was 13 and this was the first time she attended any social event that wasn't a family event. Some of my students even went on the three-day eighth-grade trip. For many of them it was the first time they had been away from home. Some had never even slept anywhere but in their own home. Another reason it was a good idea for me to become active in school activities was that the students in the general education program got to know me. Many of these kids then made a special effort to be nice to the students from my class. I know it doesn't always work this well. I guess I was lucky to be in such a supportive school.*

# Inclusion

One of the major philosophies of inclusion is that students with disabilities, who previously were viewed and treated as if they were less than others, have an opportunity to be equals with their peers. Inclusion advocates feel that educators working in inclusion programs must celebrate the strengths of the disabled students and accommodate their needs in a manner that doesn't strip the student of their dignity. "It should be stressed that in inclusive communities everyone's gifts and talent, including those of students traditionally defined as having profound disabilities or chronically disruptive behaviors, are recognized, encouraged, and used to the fullest extent possible. This occurs because each person is an important and worthwhile member with responsibilities and a role to play in supporting others. This helps foster self-esteem, pride in accomplishments, mutual respect, and a sense of belonging and self-worth among community members. This cannot occur if certain students are always receiving and never giving support" (Stainback and Stainback 1994, p.4). For many such advocates this means educating all students with disabilities in general education classroom environments. The understanding and acceptance of this philosophy is perhaps the most important aspect of preparation for an inclusion program. The educational team working with the included student must understand and agree with this philosophy or the results could be calamitous. Irreparable emotional and academic damage can occur. "The successful ones [inclusive classrooms] tend to focus on students being secure, accepted, and friends of the teacher and students, while developing feelings of belonging, positive self-worth, and success. In some cases, the primary goal is for the student to be accepted by his or her peers and teachers while developing friendships and supportive relationships. The focus on predefined curricular goals for some students is not a priority until acceptance and friendship development is addressed; although, major efforts are made to keep them actively involved with their peers in classroom activities. Gradually, as students become accepted, ways are worked out for them to be involved in classroom activities that address daily life, academic, and vocational objectives. The classrooms and schools that are unsuccessful with full inclusion tend to focus almost exclusively on assessing previously excluded students' competencies in daily life, academic and vocational skills, and designing specific curricular objectives and activities for students (regardless of what a particular student is interested in or is secure doing). They also put too little emphasis on relationships, acceptance and friendships." (Stainback, Stainback and Moravec 1994, p.61).

As previously mentioned, confusion between mainstreaming/integration and inclusion often occurs. For preparation to have the maximal effect, the distinction between the two must be made. Stainback and Stainback (1994) stated, "Integration or mainstreaming implies a need to fit students previously excluded into an existing mainstream. In inclusive schooling, the responsibility is being placed on school personnel to arrange a mainstream that accommodates the needs of all students" (p.4). It is quite difficult to translate this very simple concept into practical use in classrooms, schools, and districtwide programs. Whatever one's opinion of inclusion, there is no doubt that if programs are not designed carefully, and major changes are not implemented in the classroom, the school and the district, the inclusionary program being implemented is doomed to failure. Failure occurs for the included student who is disabled, and failure may occur for some non-disabled students in the classroom and failure may occur for the educator. "Schools must be restructured, both physically and programmatically, to provide better access to all students and to provide educational experiences that reflect the demands of an inclusive life in the community" (Giangreco and Putnam 1991, p.248).

Theoretically, many educators agree with the concept of inclusion. It makes sense to educate everyone together; however, in the practical sense it often doesn't work. Teachers are too overloaded with numbers of students and the pressure to keep the students' tests scores up, to achieve preset standards. Teachers are asked to do more and more with less and less. This creates a backlash effect. Teachers can become so "turned off" by disastrous inclusion attempts that they want nothing to do with it. Class sizes of 15 with two full-time teachers would accommodate a greater number of opportunities for inclusion of students with disabilities. Those who argue that having smaller class sizes with two adults will cost too much money can be answered by replying that the greater the number of students who can be accommodated in general education classes, the more money will be

**55**

saved in special education costs. Self-contained programs cost districts an exorbitant amount of money. This is particularly true if the student is accommodated outside of the home school or outside of the home district. Many of the resources, such as funding and efforts of school personnel on mainstreaming and special education, can be spent on assessing instructional needs, adapting instruction and providing support to students (Bauwens, Hourcade and Friend 1989).

For an inclusion program to work, general education teachers must see themselves as the primary teacher of the identified student, just as they are the primary teachers of all the other students in the classroom. "Within the framework of multiple supports, a crucial element of successful integration is for regular class teachers to assume ownership for education of the student with disabilities, just as they would for any other student on their class list. The ownership is vital to the development of an inclusionary climate in the classroom. From a practical standpoint, in order for the input of other school personnel to be truly supportive, the regular class teacher must play a significant role in guiding the process. Logically, whenever a student with disabilities is viewed by the teacher as someone else's primary responsibility, he or she is more likely to be socially and academically isolated within the regular class" (Giangreco and Putnam 1991, p.249).

As previously stated, extensive supports for the general education teacher and the special education/ consultant teacher are crucial for an inclusion program to be effective. "The effective inclusive classroom is not a setting where a teacher feels abandoned. It is not a classroom in which a teacher fears that she or he has inadequate training and background information to teach effectively. It is not the intrusion of special education teachers coming into the classroom dictating what and how the experienced general education teacher should teach. It is not a string of adult interruptions disrupting the continuity of educating children. Finally, it is not lowering standards or 'watering down' the curriculum to teach all students at the same level. It is a supportive, caring learning community in which every student feels accepted and where mutual on-going inservice occurs among teachers to help students succeed" (Tilton 1997, pp.16-17).

If the student and the educational staff members are frustrated and unhappy, things will deteriorate quickly. "When the expectations are not being met, the teacher and student feel frustrated. Expectations can be adjusted. Changes may not be needed for the entire class, but perhaps only for some students. Different expectations should not be equated with lowered expectations. Flexibility and accepting students' initial skill levels can be the basis for appropriate expectations. The goal is to move forward from that point" (Tilton 1997, p.28).

Without the support of administrators, the task of successful inclusion becomes almost impossible. "To achieve an inclusive culture focused on meeting the needs of all learners, it is important that school leaders make explicit the embedded values of diversity, membership, and collaboration in every aspect of their school's operation — from purchasing textbooks and computers, to the deployment of staff, to how decisions are made, to how professional development activities are structured" (Salisbury and McGregor 2002, p.272).

Many administrators ignore or provide no support for teachers who are struggling with students with behavior problems, who are included in general education programs. More specifically, many administrators want no part in dealing with students who are disabled, and who also may have behavior problems. The number one goal of that administrator becomes the removal of that student from the school. "Clearly, schoolwide or systemwide integration efforts will require the active support of district-level administrators, with school principals and special education counterparts serving as key people in school-level change" (Giangreco and Putnam 1991, p.261).

Many school principals and other school administrators feel ill prepared to deal with the extra responsibilities that come with including students with disabilities. University and college programs that prepare educational administrators must begin to provide the necessary training in this area. "As districts move to implement the provisions of recently reauthorized federal special educational policy, principals will need to be prepared to address these requirements at the building level" (Salisbury and McGregor 2002, p.272).

With all the labor-intensive curricular, instructional and structural changes that have to be made, it must be asked, "Is it worth all of this effort?" Certainly, inclusion advocates feel it is. Additionally, most educators can see the benefit of including students who are disabled into general education programs. Dipalma (1995) cited many benefits of inclusion for disabled students. These include improved learning through peer modeling and wider access to varied experiences. The student with a disability is better prepared for adult life by increased language skills and more appropriate social skills. There is an increased opportunity to develop friendships, which leads to a sense of belonging.

Other benefits cited by Dipalma (1995) were the benefits of inclusion for non-disabled children. These benefits include an increased appreciation and awareness of human differences and the recognition of the civil rights of others. Non-disabled students showed an improved learning rate through increased instructional accommodations. Additionally, non-disabled students may gain recognition of strengths in others and appreciation of different learning styles. These students also have an increased appreciation of the learning process by participating in peer tutoring. Increased motivation resulting from team building and participation in cooperative learning activities also occurs.

Tilton documented several positive attitudes needed for successful inclusion. These attitudes include the readiness of special education and general education class teachers to cooperate with each other, the willingness to share competencies as a team on behalf of pupils, the desire to be flexible with respect to class size and teaching assignments, and the recognition that social and personal development can be taught, and that they are as important as academic achievement.

There are a number of practical steps that can be taken to facilitate inclusive school and classroom communities: (1) Gain the teacher's commitment; (2) Use special education and other resources; (3) Establish an inclusive education task force (Stainback and Stainback 1994, p.4).

Tilton cites the benefits of inclusion that teachers have claimed. These include acceptance of all children, positive role models for students with special needs, increased self-confidence for all students, less classroom disruption (caused by pull-outs), more time with peers, and less emphasis on labeling students with special needs. Additional benefits include academic and social gains for students with special needs. Students who are disabled also gain an increased sense of belonging. Chances for general education students to learn how to help others, more efficient use of time for all students, better understanding of diversity for all students, and greater opportunity for individualized help also occur in the inclusionary classroom.

While there are many benefits for students and educational staff in inclusionary programs, there are disadvantages. Teachers cited specific challenges for identified and unidentified students in inclusionary programs. These challenges include increased noise level, individual needs and some IEP goals that are difficult to meet, increases in disturbances and interruptions, and inadequate space for individual needs. Additionally, some students with special needs can be excluded from some activities though physically included in the classroom. It is also difficult sometimes to modify and reach all students (Tilton 1997, p.132-133).

**60**

Often parents of included students who are disabled wish, as most parents do, for appropriate social interactions between their child and other children. It is the desire of many parents that their child will be included in day-to-day social events that occur outside of the classroom and school. Even with the best intentions and the best implementation of programs in school to support and encourage such interaction, it often doesn't occur. This can be devastating not only for the student with a disability, but for the parents of that child as well. There are very few things sadder than a parent stating that his or her child has never been invited over to another child's house.

## Classroom Modifications

No matter what type of classroom you have, modifying it for students who need modifications is a difficult task. When a student is diagnosed and classified with a disability common sense should prevail. Developing the appropriate modifications is not an easy task. If we under-modify for the student, there is a risk of creating undo frustration for that student. Under-modification involves having expectations that the student is either emotionally or cognitively unable to meet (e.g., sitting too long with a paper and pencil task, or assigning material that is at grade level, but too difficult for the student). If we over-modify for students, we give those students the message that they are not as competent as they are. Furthermore, you run the risk of those students developing a dependence on a "crutch" they do not need.

Over-modification could include not allowing a student, who is socially able, to eat in the cafeteria with peers, or having someone take notes for students who are capable of taking their own notes (Zimmerman 2001).

In the inclusive classroom, modifications can be even more complicated. The key is to provide the appropriate modifications for the student with disabilities without disrupting the educational program of all the students in the classroom. With all the constraints on educators this is a difficult task. The primary problem is that teachers do not have the time to meet with each other to develop and plan for modifications. It is very rare that teachers who need to work together have the same planning time.

Additionally, there are many responsibilities that teachers have besides planning modifications for students with disabilities. Among other tasks, they are required to grade papers and exams, call parents, and plan curriculum and instruction. "The two biggest challenges cited by teachers are time to plan and scheduling" (Tilton 1997, p.135). Possible solutions to provide the time required for planning, documented by Tilton, include having principals cover for a class and the use of floating substitute staff. Additionally, classroom teachers could pair up and take turns teaching students from both classes while the other teacher has meetings. The establishment of schoolwide late starts, or early dismissal, or monthly assemblies, which would require less supervision, could free up teachers to have meetings. Finally, teachers could schedule early or late meetings with compensation time (Tilton 1997, p.138).

# Academic Modifications

Curricular modifications needed for successful inclusion can be complicated and difficult to implement, too. "Not only must teaching strategies be designed and curriculum determined to respond to a range of student differences, but the curriculum must address the many ways in which students differ" (Sapon-Shevin 1994, p.19).

Students with disabilities, as well as other students, have different learning styles that call for different instructional styles. Basic principles for inclusive instruction include teaching diagnostically. In other words, differentiating instruction for learning style and skill and performance needs. Specifically this means teaching necessary skills; emphasizing and directly teaching vocabulary; emphasizing relevance and authentic performance; using appropriate and realistic examples and demonstrations; actively involving students; and encouraging cooperative learning. It also means teaching students the strategies for accomplishing tasks, teaching self-monitoring, teaching for mastery and providing appropriate practice and generous review. Teachers need to integrate skills and concepts throughout an inclusive curriculum; they need to build interest and enthusiasm, and guide students to develop self-management skills. This is a long list. It will require careful thought and preparation for development and implementation.

Many students can consistently organize thoughts and plans of action internally. An average student usually understands and follows the morning routine before a school day starts without needing a check-off list in a written form. Information about the routine is stored in the student's memory and when they wake up they do the things they need to do (eat breakfast, brush teeth, comb hair, get books ready, etc.) and mentally check off these tasks. For some students with disabilities waking up in the morning can be a nightmare; the student feels overwhelmed and doesn't even know where to begin. This lack of internal structure also can cause a tremendous amount of frustration, which may create a situation in which the student shuts down. Imagine waking up like this every day! Being prepared for the events of the school day and then living through it can be extremely difficult. The student can sometimes have one disaster followed by another and feel completely overwhelmed and inadequate. It is for these reasons that the student needs help in developing an "external scaffold." The external scaffold replaces, or at least compensates, to some degree, for the student's inability to organize internally. Some students need just a light framework because they are able to organize some things internally. Others will require a great deal more. As the student begins to internalize some of the routines and responsibilities, the scaffolding can be reduced. For some students, however, this will be a life-long battle, and they will require this scaffolding forever (Zimmerman 2001).

## Strategies for Creating External Scaffolding

- *Teach the student how to make a list and how to follow it.* People sometimes take for granted that making a list is easy. Some students with disabilities do not find making a list or following through on a list easy at all. Start small (no more than two or three simple tasks on a list) and then work your way up to longer and more complicated lists. It may help to start by having the student create a list for a schedule he or she already knows and follows.

- *It is important that students with disabilities understand and know how to follow a schedule.* If you need to, start with an hourly schedule then work up to daily, weekly, and monthly schedules. Students with disabilities are notorious for asking, "What time is lunch?" at 8:30 in the morning. To these students it is a legitimate and sincere question, related to their poor sense of time. It is essential for success, in the present as well as in the future, for a student with a disability to use calendars, clocks, and schedules as tools to help them follow the routines. A schedule taped to a student's desk can be very helpful. Students who have not yet learned to tell time will need a schedule with times and their representations on clock faces. Being able to follow schedules alleviates much of the stress that people with a disability have. They are aware of what is coming up and there are fewer surprises.

- *Use a homework assignment chart and a classwork assignment chart.* At first, filling this out will be the responsibility of both the student and educational staff, but eventually the student should take over the responsibility. Students will differ in terms of how long it will take before they can assume this responsibility themselves.

• *Provide a binder that has several organized sections for work to be done, homework assignment charts, and completed assignments.* It also should contain daily and weekly schedules, and names of people (where and when to find them) to talk to when there are problems. Color-coordinate the binders for easy access and insist that the student have the binder with him or her at all times. Recognize that for a significant time period after establishing the folder system, adult cueing will be necessary to keep up with the folder(s).

• *Provide one set of materials to be used in the classroom and one set of materials to be used by the student at his or her home.* Materials should include a writing implement, paper and any books the student may need. The materials used in the class should not leave the classroom. The materials used at home should not leave the house. Many students with a disability are disorganized and disheveled. They have difficulty holding onto and transporting materials. This does not signal a lack of respect for materials, but an inability to remain focused on the possession of the materials.

- *It will be useful to break up larger assignments or projects into smaller components with specific deadlines for each component.* Not only does this make a larger task less overwhelming, it provides a road map for tackling the project.

## Behavior Modifications

Dealing with the behavioral issues that some disabled students, who are included, bring into the classroom can be time-consuming and frustrating. Disruptive actions of both a minor or more serious nature are commonly experienced by teachers and can present an interruption to normal teaching and learning (Clarke, Parry-Jones, Gay and Smith 1981). Classroom disruption is becoming a grave matter as anti-social and aggressive behavior escalates in the schools. This kind of disruption is a major source of concern for school officials and society at large (Walker and Sylwester 1991). Patterson and Bank (1986) claim that the single best predictor of adolescent criminal behavior is a long-established pattern of early school anti-social behavior.

One of the primary goals of education is to provide an appropriate atmosphere in which to teach academic skills, while another important goal is to instill values to help the student successfully function in society. It is believed that both the individual and society will be served by fulfilling these goals. Dealing with the disruptive actions of students will have an impact on the actions that these students will choose in their future lives; actions that may, in turn, impact their communities and society as a whole

(Zimmerman 1998). These effects can be compounded in inclusionary programs.

The process of teaching is often interrupted by what are conceived to be disruptions. When disruptions occur, teachers and other educational staff find themselves in the role of disciplinarians. Teachers face the daily challenge of implementing educational strategies suitable for increasing student motivation to participate and for encouraging non-disruptive actions from those students. The degree to which classroom teachers are meeting this challenge has been the subject of much public debate. Professional educators agree that poorly selected and implemented disciplinary techniques have a negative influence on students and teachers. The effect on students of these inadequate disciplinary techniques is documented by the fact that discipline problems are the major cause of student referrals made by regular educators to special education (Smith and Misra 1992). Smith and Misra (1992) reported that the influence of discipline-related problems on teachers has been identified as the prime stress-producing factor in teaching.

Modifications for purposes of behavior management can include: the development of individual rules for students when needed; evaluation and modification of classroom structure against student needs; provision of quiet during intense learning times; reduction of visual distractions in the classroom; provision of a computer for written work; seat placement for the student with a disability within close proximity to teacher or staff; the use of study carrels for a student who would benefit; seating a student away from a window or doorway;

provision of an unobstructed view of the chalkboard and teacher; and, the use of both oral and printed directions presented in small steps (task analysis) (Tilton 1997, p.76).

# 10 Tips for a Positive Classroom Environment

## 1. Respect

*You must respect the student.* Students learn how to respect others when they are respected themselves.

## 2. Consistent rules and limits setting

*The student must be clear on "how far" he or she can go.* If there is no limit the student will have no idea when to stop. This can cause some significant disruptive behavior.

*Students can become extremely anxious without limits.* It is a comfort to the student to know someone is in charge who won't let things get too out of control.

*Rules should be clear and direct.* The student should understand what they are supposed to do.

*Rules should be reasonable and achievable.* Try not to set the student up for failure by asking him or her to do things of which he or she may not be capable (i.e., assigning schoolwork that is too difficult without appropriate teacher assistance or leaving an impulsive student unsupervised for long periods of time).

*There must be follow-through on consequences.* If rules are broken there must be a consequence, or these rules will be broken again. This also is true for rewarding appropriate behavior. If an agreement is made between a student and a teacher for a reward for certain behavior, the reward must be given if the student lives up to his or her end of the bargain. When follow-through is non-existent or inconsistent, students learn not to trust the adult, or worse, not take the adult seriously. It is better to have no rules at all, than to have rules on which the adult does not follow through.

### 3. Positive reinforcement

*Reinforce appropriate behavior.* Instead of the "squeaky wheel getting the grease," acknowledge students who behave appropriately.

*The rule for positive reinforcement is to deliver it often.* This is particularly true for students who tend to suffer from low self-esteem. They need to hear praise often. Keep in mind that individual students may need different amounts. Some students may prefer the praise to be public. Some want praise only when no one else is around.

*The praise you deliver should be honest, sincere, and specific.* It is better to say, "I like how you share materials with others," than to say "You are being good." Students can become resentful when they feel an adult is complimenting them to manipulate them.

### 4. Include students in decisions about behavior and discipline

*Imposing all the rules yourself, as the adult, generally is not a good idea.* Include the student. It makes that student feel like he or she is part of the plan, not the sole cause of the problem. It is better to do it <u>with</u> them, than <u>to</u> them.

*Give the student choices for behavior whenever possible.* When you want a student to stop a certain behavior ask him/her what a better behavior might be or suggest an alternative behavior that is more appropriate. Rules generated by students are adhered to more diligently.

*Including students in issues of behavior helps them to mature.* They will look more closely at their needs and monitor their behavior.

### 5. Be yourself with students

*Share yourself with the students.* They care about you and want to know who you are. Give them opportunities to show their sensitivity to you. Be open, honest and direct.

### 6. Be available emotionally and physically to students

### 7. Avoid power struggles — push and pull situations

*"Choose your battles."*

*Demonstrate compromise.*

## 8. Consequences

*Every action causes a reaction.* Students should understand that there are always consequences for behavior. There are two types of consequences:

1. Imposed consequences are consequences that would not necessarily follow in the natural environment. For example, assigning a student detention for not doing homework, or asking a student to go to time-out.

2. Natural consequences are a direct result of actions that occur within the environment. Here are two examples: When a student acts in an inappropriate manner other students may laugh at the student. When a student throws a favorite toy or game on the floor in anger and it breaks, that student loses the opportunity to play with the toy or game. Natural consequences are more meaningful to individuals; hence, they have the greater strength in effecting a behavior change.

## 9. Be good role models for students. The students will follow your lead!

## 10. Laugh as much and as often as possible

*You really cannot work and be with students unless you can appreciate the joy and humor this responsibility brings.*

When inappropriate behavior becomes chronic, the patterns of the inappropriate behavior need to be analyzed. Conducting a functional behavioral assessment/analysis is an invaluable method to do so. The purpose of functional behavioral assessment/analysis is to give equal attention to the function of a behavior, as to its form. An analysis of a problem behavior's function, in terms of its antecedents and consequences, is necessary for the selection of the most effective treatment procedures (Crawford, Brockel, Schauss and Miltenberger 1992). Inappropriate behavior is often a manner in which an individual communicates a need. By understanding the function of the communication we can alter the environment or teach substitute methods for individuals to get their needs met. Donnellan, Mirenda, Mesaros and Fassbender (1984) suggest that some of the functions of inappropriate behavior may include interactive functions such as requests for attention, social interaction, assistance, or objects. Other functions include negations such as protests, refusals, or cessation. Also declarations about events, objects, people, errors or greetings would be considered functional behavior. Inappropriate behavior can serve other functions such as escape from aversive conditions or internal stimulation. An analysis of the antecedents, behavior, and consequences (ABCs) yields information that lead to a hypothesis about why the behavior is occurring and how to deal with the behavior (Zimmerman 2000). Antecedents refer to the specific setting in which a behavior occurs. To identify the antecedents the following questions must be answered:

- Who is present when the behavior occurs?

- What is going on when the behavior occurs?

- When does the behavior tend to occur?

- When does the behavior tend not to occur?

- Where does the behavior tend to occur?

- Where does the behavior tend not to occur?

Specific antecedents could be, but are not limited to, who the individual is sitting next to, hunger, temperature of the room, subject being taught.

The consequences of behavior refer to the actions that usually follow the behavior in that setting. To identify the consequences the following questions must be answered:

- What happens after the behavior occurs?

- What do the staff members do?

- What do the other students do?

- What does the individual who engaged in the behavior do?

- What do you think increases the likelihood of the behavior occurring again?

Specific consequences could be, but are not limited to, a teacher's anger, being sent out of the room, other students laughing, a student avoids a task that he or she finds aversive. Once a functional analysis/assessment is performed, a behavior intervention plan suited to the individual can be developed and formulated.

# Chapter Five

# Consultant Teacher Model and Collaboration

In the purist form of the consultant teacher model, the student is not pulled out of the general education class at all. All services are provided within the general education classroom. The consultant teacher is a trained special education teacher who works in the classroom directly providing services to the disabled student. The consultant teacher also works with the disabled student's general education teacher to help the teacher understand how to work with the student in the general education classroom. Additionally, the consultant teacher and the general education teacher work together, sharing expertise on, among other things, issues of curriculum, instruction, and behavior management. The consultant teacher also may work with other educators who are working with the student with the disability. In the best of all possible situations the consultant teacher is part of a team that collaborates with the other educational personnel who work with the disabled student. (Collaboration will be discussed later in this chapter.)

There are various potential problems that are caused by an inappropriate use of the consultant teacher. "If the special education teacher merely 'takes over' for the

**75**

regular teacher and instructs a certain number of children for a portion of the regular teacher's day, the chances to share are diluted and the particular skills of the consulting teacher underutilized. . . .The goal is not to relieve the regular education teacher from the responsibility for teaching difficult students" (Huefner 1988, p.404).

Huefner goes on to say, "If the consulting model includes direct, substantive service to students in the regular classroom on a continuing basis, there will be pressure to turn the model into a classroom tutoring or aide model, underutilizing the consulting teacher's potential contribution to regular education programs in general" (p.407).

Research shows that there are specific supports consultant teachers can provide to general educators. General educators feel more comfortable when support from the consultant teacher consists of more than suggestions on how to accommodate the special needs of the disabled student (Fuchs, Fuchs, Bahr, Fernstrom and Stecker 1990). Interaction between the consultant teacher and the general education teacher leads to increased feeling of teacher competence (Miller and Sabatino 1978). This interaction relieves the general education teacher's apprehensive feeling about working with students who are disabled. It is typical for teachers to be more cooperative in the inclusion process when they have this type of support.

As previously noted, the need for consistent and ongoing support between general educators and special educators, is essential for an effective consultative relationship to exist. Unfortunately, available evidence suggests that in practice, an inadequate amount of time, lack of administrative support and lack of preparation threaten the integrity of this form of support (McGregor and Vogelsberg 1998). This has become a major concern for all teachers, whether they are special education or general education teachers. Teachers become frustrated and become less cooperative when they do not have time built into the day to collaborate and consult.

The term "consultant" can create negative presumptive connotations for the general education teacher. Consultant often refers to an "expert." This can rub an experienced general educator the wrong way. "Most consultative models are based on the presumption that the consultant is an expert who brings specialized information to a problematic situation. In a school setting, this creates a hierarchical relationship between the special and general educator, in which the expectation is that the general educator is ready, willing, and able to implement recommendations made by the specialist. Evidence indicates that this in not always the case" (McGregor and Vogelsberg 1998, p.46). One of the responses to the dissatisfaction with the term "consultant teacher" is to use a more expanded and accurate term — collaborative consultation. This term implies an equal relationship between team members.

When a consultant teacher has minimal experience or less experience than the general education teacher the problem of credibility is often magnified. To achieve credibility, a consultant teacher should have at least five years experience as a classroom teacher. At times, recent graduates of special education programs with either a bachelor's or master's degree, who have not had previous teaching experience, are placed in the consultant teacher position. If the consultant teacher has not had classroom experience, he or she may be unable to understand the day-to-day experience the general educator has, and this may create a situation where the consultant makes unrealistic suggestions to the general education teacher. Even if the consultant teacher is excellent at this position, if he or she is new to the field of education, or if he or she has never had classroom experience, it is difficult for a veteran general education teacher to accept the consultant or the recommendations and suggestions that the consultant teacher may make.

Problems also can surface between the special education/consultant teacher and the general education teacher even if both are highly experienced. It is suggested by Johnson, Pugach and Hammitte (1988) that dissonance can exist due to the special educator's lack of credibility relative to the general education classroom, mismatches between the thinking of the special education consultant and classroom teacher, the hierarchical nature of the consultative relationship, and the differing knowledge bases of general and special educators. Without a positive, cooperative, and supportive relationship between the general education teacher and the special education/ consultant teacher the best-designed inclusion program will not work.

Dr. Georgette Albert was a special education teacher for eight years and worked as a behavioral consultant for seven years. Dr. Albert is currently a special education training specialist who works with educational staff members and has been involved in inclusion advocacy for more than 15 years. She belongs to a parent and educator inclusion council and, in the past, has served as the council's president. Dr. Albert points out —

> *People who wanted to have more inclusion opportunities for more students jumped on the consultant teacher model. Parents wanted to have their kids involved in this.*

There are requisites for the consultation model to work, Dr. Albert said.

> *I think the "A number one" thing is good solid training for administrators. They need to understand why this is a workable model. They need to be provided good inservice to show them that kids do better, and I don't mean just the kids with disabilities. Kids without disabilities also benefit. It's positive on both sides. We need to help administrators sell the model and then we need to provide staff development for everybody — the teachers, paraprofessionals, related service providers . . . really everybody so they understand how to make this model work. We also need to do good decision-making in terms of which students should go with which teachers. Sometimes the model has been killed because of the way it was set up. Then everybody gets a really bad taste in his or her mouth. Once that happens it's*

> *hard to come back. In order for this to work, it requires a great deal of trust between people. It requires an ability to accept the other person's philosophy of education and an ability to kind of get rid of some of the "turf issues." In the ideal situation, you can't really tell who the special education teacher is and who the general education teacher is. It's been my experience that only about 15 percent of the teachers can actually carry that off.*

What role should the consultant teacher take with the general education teacher? Dr. Albert adds:

> *In the most ideal situation, the special education teacher team teaches with the general education teacher. I have seen some marvelous examples of that. There are several models of team teaching including both teachers up there teaching at the same time and trading off. Also, one teacher could be wandering around supporting the students while the other teaches. The teachers can alternate their roles day by day.*

What are some of the difficulties associated with the consultant model?

> *The consultant model was originally intended, primarily, for students who had mild disabilities. The staffing levels are*

*unrealistic if this model is used for stu-
dents who have more severe disabilities. It
[the consultant teacher model] can work
very well with students who have severe
disabilities, but there has to be an understanding on the part of people making
staffing decisions, that if a teacher is
working with a student with a severe disability, you can't give that teacher a full
caseload of 20 students. The decision
about caseloads for consultant teachers is
really important. People need to be realistic about what can be done within the time
frame. If you think about kids in high
school they might have six or seven different teachers. It's not realistic to give a
consultant teacher 20 kids.*

Dr. Albert said there are other roadblocks that get in
the way of successful inclusion.

*Way too often the administration has not
been real clear on what its intention is. The
general education teacher doesn't know
what the special education teacher is supposed to be doing. On the other hand,
sometimes the general education teacher is
not willing to turn anything over to the special education teacher. He or she ends up
treating the special education teacher like
a paraprofessional. So the consultant
teacher ends up in the classroom aimlessly,*

**81**

*not doing anything that a teaching assis-
tant couldn't do. It's particularly difficult
for new teachers who are hired as consult-
ants and have never done it before. They
kind of get sucked into "the dark side,"
because they don't know how it's supposed
to be. It's very difficult.*

Emma Johnson has been a special education/
consultant teacher for five years. Ms. Johnson also has
experience as a classroom teacher that includes both
teaching as a general education teacher and as a special
education teacher. Currently, Ms. Johnson has a caseload
of eight students who have a variety of disabilities. The
grade level of the students she teaches is between
kindergarten and high school, with students ranging in age
from 5 to 16 years old. Her caseload requires her to travel
to different schools during the course of each day. Here is
her take on the consultant teacher model at work in the
included classroom.

*I think the consultant teacher model is
much better than the resource room model.
When there is a resource room, other students can look in and think, "Well, I know
what they're doing in there." The disadvantages of the consultant teacher model is
that the consultant teacher spends a lot of
time chasing teachers down and figuring
out what's going on in the classroom.*

Ms. Johnson does encounter some logistical problems
as a special education/consultant teacher.

*One of the biggest problems is that you're not able to be a team member all the time. I only come into each class for a limited time during the week. I think to be the most effective you would need to be able to see what goes on all the time and then be able to assist in that way. Not only students, but also teachers would see you as someone who is always involved in what is happening, and not just as someone coming in and doing a piece and leaving. That's probably one of the biggest problems.*

Ms. Johnson said many of the students she works with need assistance in so many areas. She sometimes finds it difficult making choices as to what instructional and curricular path she should take.

*The next biggest problem is trying to figure out where you're needed most to serve the student best. These students are almost always behind in work, and you could easily spend the entire time of your job keeping them caught up with work. By the same token, you need to get them caught up in the study skills they need to get through, then you throw in the whole exam piece. You can clearly spend most of your time with some students prepping them for exams . . . especially at the high school level. It is difficult to allocate my time to do all of those things [catching students up with work tasks, teaching them study skills, and exam preparation] effectively because all of these things are so badly needed. As a special education teacher I see these huge skill deficits that I would really like to spend my time catching students up with, and at the same time the student is taking a practice biology regents exam and scoring 25 percent. You know they have to get through that, and everyone is looking at you and saying, "get them through this," but he can't very well get through the test if he's not reading or writing well. It's hard to figure out how much time I need to spend on each thing to get the student where they need to be. It gets to be crazy. Everyone is pulling in different directions.*

Ms. Johnson also knows the time-constraint pressures the general education teacher has in terms of meeting with the consultant teacher and doing the extra paper work that is required when you have students with disabilities in your room.

*One of the problems that faces general education teachers is that students in their class who are disabled require more work for the teacher, and that's how the teacher sees it. I feel that many general education teachers wouldn't do it [have students with disabilities in their classes] if they weren't required to do it. When you have these four or five students who need you [general education teacher] to fill out IEP goals, objectives, and benchmarks and these types of things, it takes extra time.*

Developing a positive relationship with the general education teachers can be difficult. Ms. Johnson feels if the general education teacher were given release time, or paid for the extra work required, the level of cooperation would increase.

*Working with another professional can be intimidating, and it can be threatening. As much as you try to make it not threatening and not tell the teacher what to do, it can still be so hard. After all, part of my job, as a consultant teacher, is to tell the teacher what I think they should do. It's not that anyone is necessarily a bad teacher. It's just that sometimes the teacher is not thinking about something in particular for that student and that student needs that accommodation. It's not something that the teacher would pick out. In a lot of cases you're [the consultant teacher] with these kids for three or four years. When the kid gets a new teacher, you do know more about that kid. This can create a threatening situation for them. There's a "turf issue" and then there's the thought —"I have enough to do without sitting with you for an hour every week and talking to you about one student. I have one hundred students." I understand that it's hard for them to justify that time with me when they have a hundred kids.*

Providing consultant teacher services as a "push-in" service sometimes can present problems, she said. (Push-in services are the opposite of pull-out services. Students receive services in the general education class in a push-in situation. Pull-out services require taking the student out of the general education class and providing the service in a separate location.)

*I have better luck doing push-in services at the elementary level . . . kindergarten through sixth-grade. It's virtually impossible to do it [push-in services] in a high school classroom. I have tried it, and it is so upsetting for the high school students I work with at the high school level to have me there in their general education classes. It doesn't matter what I'm doing or how I have been introduced to the student and the class. The disabled student and the other students very clearly know whom I'm there for. Even if they (the disabled student[s]) likes me very much. Push-in works much better when I can spend a great deal of time in the general education class. When I'm there for a longer time I can focus on other kids. It helps the student [who is dis-*

*abled] and the other students see me as just another adult that will help all of them.*

Obstacles can occur if the general education teacher does not understand the role and purpose of the consultant teacher.

*The teacher will often treat you as a para-professional. It gets crazy. I've been asked to wipe off tables and take kids who have misbehaved out into the hall. You feel terrible having to constantly reassert your role, but you have to. If you don't, you end up doing all these things that you're not there for. It can get very difficult, and you can get into a confrontational situation. I think a lot of people don't understand the consultant teacher model. I also think that many teachers don't understand how to team-teach with anybody else. I do see how difficult it can be to have other professionals in the room. When you come into the room as a professional, you have an agenda and you have goals and objectives to meet. This doesn't always match the classroom teacher's goals and objectives.*

All in all, Ms. Johnson concluded, the consultant teacher model works. She feels it is the best way, at this time, to provide appropriate educational programming for students with disabilities who are included in general education classes.

## Collaboration

It is well documented that the preparation and implementation for a successful inclusion program requires a great degree of cooperation and collaboration. If the student has many needs and a number of service providers, it is beneficial and highly recommended that the IEP should include a provision for all service providers to get together on a regular basis to coordinate. "Inclusion requires effective collaboration among the adults who are teaching together in an atmosphere of mutual on-going inservice" (Tilton 1997, p.22). Collaboration ensures program consistency and also provides much needed support for all service providers.

A team approach is necessary to make sure that all the facets of the student's programs are being implemented and monitored. Team members can include, but are not limited to, the following individuals: special educators, general educators, parents, students, administrators, school psychologists, school counselors, social workers, speech-language therapists, physical therapists, occupational therapists, adaptive physical education teachers, vocational teachers, school nurses, outside medical personnel, educational assistants, bus drivers, lunch monitors, and community resources.

Collaboration provides the educational team working with an included student who is disabled an opportunity to learn from the expertise of others and to share individual expertise. Collaboration also provides those most involved with the student, opportunities for "having a say" in the development and implementation of an appropriate and beneficial program. "Collaboration is the process of a team of individuals working together to create opportunities for students to learn. Collaboration is really about interpersonal relationships. It involves the partnership between many people to facilitate the implementation of inclusion. While most collaboration for the daily education of a particular student occurs on a teacher-to-teacher basis, many of these individuals listed will likely be involved, at some point, in planning for students and will function as critical members of the collaborative team. Inevitably, when dealing with an issue as complex as inclusion, the communication process and relationship among team members determine success or failure in effectively planning for students" (Tilton 1997, p.128-129).

During the collaborative process, consensus is vital. It only takes one staff member to undermine a potentially successful and valuable program. Ownership by each member of the team increases the likelihood of a program that meets the needs of the student. "Too often, the team concept, which is mandatory in the evaluation, program, and placement functions of IDEA, becomes translated in practice into the teacher assuming all the logistical and paperwork duties" (Bateman 1995, p.87). Others must share in the burden, and team members need to support each other. The dynamics of the relationship between educational staff members are integral.

"Collaboration consultation may be one excellent service delivery model, but research and experience suggest that its success depends on two individuals having a chemistry and good transactions — a chemistry that is difficult to define and that occurs rarely and transactions with uncertain effects on students" (Kauffman and Hallahan 1995, p.15). Open and honest communication in this process is requisite. "Too often, too little time is devoted to developing a relationship based on communication which is open, honest and comfortable" (Tilton 1997, p.130). Communication breakdowns are one of the major reasons why inclusion programs fail. "In order to facilitate inclusive education, the staff involved should work toward these goals: communication, flexibility, modifying instruction, preparation, commitment, and positive attitude" (Dipalma 1995, p.21). Learning is enhanced by the increased assistance provided by multiple members of a team of educators and support personnel.

In discussing the process by which educators work to develop, implement, and evaluate the adaptations that will occur in classrooms, Graden and Bauer (1994) discuss two principles which they find to be basic to the process. The first principle is that "it must be collaborative — educators must work together as equal partners not in a hierarchy to provide learning opportunities" (p.85). The second principle is that "it must be based on a specific problem-solving sequence to provide a mechanism for deciding when and how to make adaptations. Collaborative problem-solving provides the support network by which interventions, adaptations, and accommodations are implemented in inclusive classrooms" (p.85).

Collaboration includes implementing a clear plan with specific roles assigned to the members of the team.

Team members feel comfortable when their roles are clearly delineated and when they know the roles of the other members on the team.

One of the biggest obstacles to successful collaboration is lack of adequate time for educational staff members to collaborate. There are some possible remedies. Mary Anne Raywide (1993) outlined some broad approaches for creating time for collaboration: "The time can be found by: taking time from that now scheduled for other things (instruction or staff development, for instance); adding additional time to the school day and/or the school year; or altering staff utilization patterns so that all administrators regularly do some teaching, for instance, or so that some teachers assume responsibility for more youngsters while other teachers meet."

Tilton (1997) cited the top complaints teachers have concerning collaboration. These complaints include a lack of sufficient planning time, scheduling difficulties, a lack of adequate training, personality and teaching style differences, "turfism," a lack of needed administrative support, insufficient space, communication issues, increased noise levels, disruption of classroom routines and resistance to change (p.134).

Tilton (1997) documented five program requirements for successful collaboration. These include "administrative support, pre-planning before implementation, parent involvement, a view of collaboration as an on-going process — not an event and a time and place to meet on a regular basis" (p.145).

Dr. Albert, who previously discussed the consultant teacher model, also knows the importance of collaboration.

*The purpose of collaboration is that old synergy thing. When you get two heads together, assuming they're both sane and willing to participate together, things only get better. When you have collaboration between teachers you have less burnout. You have more creative programming, and you model what you want kids to do. We live in a collaborative society. People are very rarely able to get jobs where they don't have to collaborate. If we can have collaboration that is transparent so the kids can see how collaboration happens that would be very positive for them. I think the idea of being "part of the team" keeps people more open to change.*

Why isn't collaboration always successful? Dr. Albert explains:

*Collaboration is damned hard. It's extremely difficult. Part of it has to do with issues of trust. Also, general education teachers who have been successful over the years doing things without collaboration find it hard to accept that they should collaborate. The other thing is that collaboration is very time-intensive. You get a better product, but it takes longer. The process is tedious and time-consuming, and teachers don't have that much time. I think one of the things that happens is that sometimes teachers feel that they have to collaborate on everything. They end up killing themselves.*

Dr. Albert suggests ways to improve the collaborative process.

*I think at the pre-service level we need to provide student teachers with a class and a practicum on the collaboration piece. They need to know how to go into a classroom and collaborate without making that other person feel bad. I think when it is working well we need to celebrate. Administrators need to be out in the building. An administrator's desk and chair should be dusty.We need follow-up support. We need job-imbedded support. We need to set up more opportunities for mentoring so teachers can have strong, positive role models.*

As previously mentioned, it is essential for teachers, educational assistants and other staff members to work in a collaborative and amicable manner. Some teams work wonderfully well together. Some teams have to work at being cohesive. Not having clearly delineated responsibilities for staff members can create an uncomfortable working relationship and cause tension. Responsibilities for educational assistants, and other educational staff members will be different in every classroom. It is important for all the members of the educational team to discuss responsibilities and to have an understanding of how the responsibilities will be carried out. Communication is essential. If one person is unhappy, uncomfortable, or dissatisfied, it is that person's responsibility to speak up. The following is a list of tips to assist the team in collaborating and cooperating with each other.

## Tips for Effective Teamwork

- Team members should respect each other and the respective jobs each individual member does.

- Always try to think of the other person's point of view.

- Always back up other team members in front of the student(s).

- Do not discuss problems between yourselves in front of the class or student(s).

- Plan specific times to meet and plan as needed.

- Always try to keep lines of communications open.

- If you are a teacher, inform the other team members of long-term and immediate changes in the program.

- If you are a team member, accept a teacher's need to spontaneously change a day's activities.

- If you are a team member, share with the teacher important confidential information you may come across.

- Do not, if you are a teacher, leave your classroom without providing instructions or plans.

- If you are a team member, understand the need of the teacher to sometimes leave the classroom.

- All team members should appropriately handle the "personal baggage" they bring into the classroom.

- Share with the classroom students the things that are going on, particularly changes in routines.

# Chapter Six

# Educational Assistants

In many cases, students with special needs in mainstreamed or inclusionary programs are assigned an educational assistant. "Teacher aides or educational assistants have been used extensively to support students with disabilities placed in regular classes" (Giangreco and Putnam 1991, p.260). In fact, the numbers of educational assistants hired since the 1980s have soared. "The size of the paraeducator workforce continues to climb as schools and districts place more students with disabilities in programs alongside their peers without disabilities" (Pickett 1999).

Decisions for assigning a one-to-one educational assistant are numerous. Freschi (1999) documented some of the justifications for the use of a one-to-one educational assistant for a student with disabilities who, for part of the day, or all of the day, is in general education classes. One-to-one educational assistants are used in the initial transition period into an integrated setting. They are used for communication support and assistance in managing behavioral problems. They also are used to ensure general safety for both the student with special needs and that student's classmates.

The role of the educational assistant has often been ambiguous, without clearly defined parameters. The actual job title of educational assistant does not even have

**97**

a consistent name. Individuals in these roles sometimes are referred to as teacher aides, paraprofessionals, paraeducators, educational aides, teacher assistants and monitors, as well as other names.

There are various ways in which the educational assistant delivers educational support: Dipalma (1995) documents five models of paraprofessional support: (1) one-to-one direct support shared; (2) direct support; (3) indirect support; (4) faded support; and (5) variable support (p.22). "Service delivery patterns for the use of teacher aides has followed three basic patterns: (1) one aide is assigned to one student full time; (2) one aide is assigned to a small group of students within the same class or school (typically, two to four students); or (3) two or more aides rotate responsibilities for both direct student support and other school duties such as library support, bus supervision" (Giangreco and Putnam 1991, p.260).

The relationship between the student and educational assistant is vital. There is a delicate balance between appropriate and inappropriate assistance. The educational assistant must be cautious not to create or contribute to the students' over-dependence.

In addition, there are other problems that can arise. "Some parents and professionals have expressed concern that the assignment of aides may result in a situation where the least trained of the adults involved with the student has the most responsibility and may often be left to make many day-to-day decisions. Others are concerned that the over-reliance on teacher aides interferes with the development of a sense of ownership of the regular classroom teacher for a student with severe disabilities who has a one-to-one aide assigned" (Giangreco and Putnam 1991, p.260).

Recent research on the role of the educational assistants in the inclusionary setting yielded some alarming results. Educational assistants often assume too much responsibility for the student, bond with students to the point of becoming overprotective, inadvertently interfere with the student's social interaction goals, and are viewed by parents and educators as the student's primary teacher (Downing, Ryndak and Clark 2000; French and Chopra 1999). This is not the intention of educational assistant use. Measures must be taken to prevent these things from occurring. It is clear, at the very least, the educational assistant needs the supervision and support of the teacher and, perhaps, other members of the team. Specifically, one-to-one educational assistants need to know exactly what they are supposed to do. Many of these aides when hired are only given general guidelines and are never given any explicit job expectations. Additionally, it is common for one-to-one educational assistants to have no knowledge or limited knowledge of the specific disability the student they are working with may have.

As documented by Mueller (1997), high turnover rates are an additional dilemma. Educational assistants, with little training, burn out from the increased reliance on them as the sole resource for implementing complex student programs. It also should be pointed out that most educational assistants are minimally paid, which drives them to leave their positions, sometimes in the middle of a school year, which is distressing for the student and the educational staff.

Educational assistants require support and direction. Without this, an educational assistant may feel lost and frustrated. "The intent is to provide teams with a structure that requires team members to address alternative or natural supports. These supports are important to ensure quality peer interactions that facilitate a sense of belonging, enhance actual student learning, and promote incipient friendships — the cornerstones of effective and successful inclusion" (Mueller and Murphy 2001, p.26). Since many team meetings occur during the school day the one-to-one educational assistant is often excluded. Districts rarely pay one-to-one educational assistants for extra time spent at team meetings held before or after school.

Training for the educational assistant is also extremely important. Training should include information about the individual student with whom the assistant will be working, as well as information about the specific disability that the student may have.

To provide the proper support and structure, Mueller and Murphy (2001) suggest a plan that includes all the team members. "What follows is a decision-making model that attempts to have all stakeholders on the same page and focused on goals that are objectively determined. Its focus is to determine the role of the paraeducator in relation to (1) the specific support needs of the student; (2) how independence can be progressively furthered; (3) what natural supports are to be used to support the student; (4) how social acceptance can be increased" (p.26).

Often one-to-one educational assistants are required to deal with more than one teacher. This is particularly true at the secondary-school level. With different teachers running classrooms differently, applying different styles, the assistant may become confused and frustrated. Each teacher may have different expectations for the same student or different ideas of what the one-to-one educational assistant's role or tasks should be. Much of this confusion can be eradicated by having individual teachers define what their expectations are. It is important for teachers to identify their preferences to prevent potential misunderstandings. Teachers should inform their assistants of what the classroom rules are and what consequences should be applied for student misbehavior.

Additionally, teachers should state what they would like the one-to-one educational assistant to do when students, other than the student they are assigned, break the rules or otherwise misbehave. For instance, it should be made clear what the procedure is for handling misbehavior issues, like who should intervene, the teacher or the adult nearest the situation. One-to-one educational assistants also need to know what the positive consequences for appropriate behavior are and whether the teacher prefers to be the one who dispenses positive consequences. One purpose of education is to help students become more independent. This is true for children who have one-to-one educational assistants, just as it is for other students. Therefore, one part of the role of an assistant is to "fade" support from the target student as much as possible while maintaining the level of support necessary for maximum benefit. Teachers should discuss with the assistant what kinds of activities to engage in during "fading" times (e.g., answering the

**101**

questions of other students, checking work, or grading papers).

A plan for fading the educational assistant's support should be built into the initial plan. A good way to start the fading process is to have the assistant work with other students. "The aide's scheduled time should be spent both with the individual child and other children. It is important that the aide work with other children in the class. This helps with fading and the use of natural supports" (Freschi 1999, p.44). The added benefit to having the assistant work with other students is that the student with special needs sees that he or she is not the only student requiring assistance. Likewise, the other students in the class see this as well. O'Brien and Forrest (1989) provide the following advice on how to address fading with your educational assistant. "Discuss the role of the student's assistant if the student needs one. Make it clear that the assistant's job is to fade direct help to encourage other students to get involved with the new [included] student. Discuss contributions the assistant might be able to make to the whole class. From the beginning, avoid the idea that the assistant has responsibility for the student with special needs, while the teacher has responsibility for the rest of the students in the class" (p.33).

Another good strategy is to have the teacher and educational assistant switch roles from time to time. This will give both educators the opportunity "to individually experience and understand problems, challenges, techniques, and strategies, and helps reduce the dependency on the child's part" (Freschi 1999, p.45).

Debbie Herman has been a one-to-one educational assistant in a suburban elementary school for three and a half years. She has worked with students who have been diagnosed with Attention Deficit Disorder, Attention Deficit Hyperactivity Disorder, and Asperger Syndrome. Additionally, she has worked with students who have been labeled emotionally disturbed. Although Ms. Herman works in a school district that has a good reputation, it is clear that there are many deficiencies in how educational assistants are used, trained, and supported. She said she became an aide because she wanted to do something that had meaning.

> *I was at home with kids for 10 years and I thought I had so much meaning in their lives that I wanted to continue that. I wanted to make a difference.*

After becoming an educational assistant she realized the scope of her responsibilities.

> *When I'm inside the classroom I keep an eye on the students to make sure that they're on task. If they have a question or problem, I will address it. Sometimes students who are emotionally disturbed ask for help when they don't really need it or the other way around. So I keep an eye on what's going on. I pick them up from the bus. Sometimes I have to kind of yank them from Mom's arms if they're getting dropped off and they don't want to come to school. I do a lot of checking in and out through the course of the day to*

**103**

*help them get organized. I meet them and go through the backpack and getting unpacked to make sure they have their homework and that their homework is handed in. That would be at the beginning of the day. At the end of the day it would be just the reversed . . . making sure that they know what their assignments are and getting them all set up to do that assignment. I go on the playground with the kids sometimes. I eat with them in the cafeteria at lunch. I go to music. I go to gym. I go right into the locker room when they have gym. Whenever there is a potential for a problem I go.*

Although Ms. Herman is closely involved with the students, she is not included in team decisions about them. But she does try to speak up for them.

*I'm an aide. I don't have a college degree. Some teachers will ask for input, but I'm not invited to meetings. I don't think the teachers realize that they don't know a couple of the aspects of the child. So as a one-on-one aide I'm trying to work on being a better advocate for that child . . . speaking up, even when you haven't been asked and saying it anyway. "So and so might be having a problem because of this . . ."*

Ms. Herman said she becomes frustrated by not being included in the meetings and that she also would benefit from additional supports.

*I would like to see all the aides get together to support each other. We try to get that going every year, but it's just not working. We definitely need more training. I also think the aides need more supervision. I'm alone with these kids a lot, and they [teachers] don't know what I am doing. I do all these behavioral plans, but no one knows about them. I run them by Nancy [school social worker], but not all of my kids see the social worker. I'm totally on my own. I think the classroom teachers need to follow through a little more on what I'm doing. I know the teachers are stretched to their limit, but there's just not enough communication. There's no time. When the teachers have their planning time, I'm up with the student. I don't have that time to talk with the teacher.*

Even though Ms. Herman is a paraprofessional she is expected to perform other tasks. Some of these tasks do not relate to the student with whom she is working. She explained that it is not her responsibility to discipline other students, but "the teachers expect it."

*I am sometimes asked to pull other students and work with them in the hall or in the library, even though I'm supposed to be with my student. That has always occurred in every class I've ever been in. There is a lot of clerical work the teachers ask us to do. There's [photocopying], putting up bulletin boards, taking down bulletin boards . . . and that's time away from being in the classroom. That can be a problem. On the other hand, if I free up the teacher a little bit she's free to help that student, so that student isn't totally dependent on me. So it has a negative and a positive.*

What would Ms. Herman change to make the one-to-one educational assistant job more effective?

*I think the one-to-one aides have to be handpicked for each child. We also need more training. I have no psychology background. I was a stockbroker before I did this. I feel, especially this year, that there is a lot going on with this child that I'm with, and I'm not qualified to handle that.*

Ms. Herman referred to a specific student she works with —

*She [the student] sees a specialist, once a week, for an hour. She sees a social worker for a half-hour. These are the people that are trained. She has a lot of issues. I don't feel as an aide that I know enough. I think there should be an aide-mentoring program. Nobody has told me what I'm supposed to do as the aide. It's from teacher to teacher. The teacher would say, "this is the student"*

*and then very briefly tell you what to do.*
*You sort of make it up as you go along.*

## Summary

For educational assistants to be most beneficial, certain conditions should exist. Assistants should be oriented to both the position and to the school climate. They also should be trained so that they will have the necessary knowledge about the individual students they are working with and the specific disabilities the students may have. It is requisite that the educational assistants have a comprehensive job description with a clear understanding of who will supervise them.

Additionally, the educational assistant must be considered part of the staff and team. There must be adequate time to meet with the classroom teacher and other team members to schedule and plan. An environment that fosters open communication is essential. The educational assistant must be considered a valued team member and recognized for his or her contributions.

Educational assistants will be most successful when certain strategies are employed. They must listen to students and take time to find out about their day. The assistant should assist all students in the classroom so that a student with a disability does not become overly dependent when it is not necessary. They should reinforce the same approach the teacher uses in explaining concepts in order to maintain consistency. When there is a difference of opinions between the educational assistant and the teacher, it must be discussed privately, not in front of students. The educational assistant must respect students and staff members and expect respect in return. The assistant should not make unilateral decisions about the student's program if those decisions are not in agreement with the educational plan in place. It is always beneficial for the assistant to build on the past success of the students and to help students discover strengths.

Assistants should praise students by citing specific accomplishments and accept students at current performance levels. It helps for the assistant to maintain a sense of humor and enjoy time spent with students, to develop a trust level with them, and to support students who feel insecure or unsure. Educational assistants should always try to encourage students to work independently, fading one-to-one time as appropriate and, as often as possible, giving attention and concern to all the students in the classroom and providing extra attention when the teacher is busy. It will always be imperative that the assistant model patience and stability. Reinforcement of positive behavior and, perhaps the most important thing, celebrating success, will surely be beneficial to the student.

# Chapter Seven

# Case Study

Jonathon Rebilog is an 11-year-old boy who has Asperger Syndrome. The fifth-grader is in an inclusion program in his home district elementary school. In fourth-grade, Jonathon was in a fully included class. This was not a successful year for him. Most of his lack of success was due to a poorly designed and implemented inclusion program. At the end of his fourth-grade year, a decision was made to have Jonathon repeat the year with the same teacher. The second year in fourth-grade was highly successful for Jonathon. Much of this success was attributed to a well-designed and well-implemented inclusion program in which many educators, and Jonathon's parents, participated.

Jonathon was adopted at birth. His mother has a degree in human services and has experience working with individuals with disabilities. She was a floor supervisor for 13 years at a sheltered workshop and currently tutors special education students at the elementary level for the school district her son attends. Mrs. Rebilog explained Jonathon's background.

*I believed early that there was something going on with this child. There was a lot of crying as a baby. I noticed when he*

**109**

*became a toddler there was not a lot of interaction with other children. There was a lot of isolated play . . . wanting to be alone. When other kids would approach him he would leave. I kept mentioning it to the pediatrician. Her thoughts were, "You're a nervous first mom." Family members and friends were telling me I couldn't possibly have an intuition because I didn't have a biological connection. But I knew something wasn't right and I finally insisted, when he was 3 years old, that we have an evaluation. He was diagnosed with Pragmatic Language Disability. By that time he had been politely kicked out of two nursery schools. He would leave group situations. Free playtime was fine because he would parallel play. He was very quiet . . . pretty much not talking, unless he wanted something badly enough. When it came time for circle time or story time he would refuse to sit with the group. A language-based nursery school was recommended by the pediatric developmental specialist.*

After looking at several programs, Mrs. Rebilog chose a pre-school that specialized in Applied Behavior Analysis. It was an intensive program where the staff worked on all of Jonathon's deficit areas including toilet training. Mrs. Rebilog reported that Jonathon made "leaps and bounds with progress." When it was time for kindergarten, Jonathon went to an integrated program in his home school district. It was a half-day program, as were all the kindergarten classes in this district. It was not his home school, but the only school that had an integrated program in Jonathon's home school district.

> *I didn't really like it. I thought that it would be too restrictive for Jonathon. The children there seemed needier than him . . . at least academically. We did stay there, and it was good for him. He seemed to be happy in the program. I didn't particularly care for it. At about mid year, I asked to have Jonathon spend some time in the afternoon kindergarten, which was not integrated, . . . extend his day. Everybody was reluctant to do that. I think the afternoon kindergarten teacher's fear was, "They're telling me this kid has all these problems in the integrated program. How can we possibly expect him to do well here?" I really loved the integrated kindergarten teacher. She was a warm, loving and protective teacher, but she didn't want to let go. The building principal was not supportive. I had to use pressure by saying things like, "I cannot believe you people would not allow this child to break out of special education and be challenged." Finally the principal said, "We will try this a couple of days a week for a couple of hours." After one week I asked the afternoon kindergarten teacher how Jonathon*

*was doing. She told me he was doing just
fine. We decided to have him attend
through the end of the day. Jonathon went
through the rest of the year attending both
the integrated program in the morning and
the regular kindergarten program in the
afternoon, Monday through Friday, successfully.*

Mrs. Rebilog saw the difference between the
integrated program and the general education program in
the work her son was bringing home:

*Anyone who says that there's not a differ-
ence between an integrated classroom and
a regular classroom is totally out of their
mind. The integrated classroom is geared
probably toward the level of the lower or
mediocre student within that classroom.
Jonathon was bringing home artwork and
pictures and coloring from the integrated
class and in the regular class he was
counting money and learning organiza-
tional skills and words. There was a major
difference so I was really glad that I pur-
sued that.*

Jonathon remained in his home school district for
first-grade and, in fact, attended his home school. He
received speech therapy, physical therapy, and consultant
teacher services as pull-out and push-in supports. During
the middle of the year it was decided that Jonathon also
required a full-time educational assistant.

*In first-grade Jonathon went to Buckman Elementary School because that was his home school. After three days of school the teacher told me that he would not be able to attend any of the field trips and that I was going to have to come to school everyday to get his folder out of his backpack because he was incapable. I requested that she say, "Jonathon get your folder out of your backpack." She told me "absolutely not, that would take too much time away from the other children." He was out of that classroom in three days. I just knew that this was a personality that wasn't going to work well for Jonathon. She was not welcoming of any child that didn't "fit into the track." Jonathon started in another first-grade class in the building. His new teacher was very warm and welcoming. She was open and willing to accept anyone into her class and willing to do whatever it takes, but really didn't have an understanding of Jonathon and his unique needs. I'll never forget a comment she made. She said, "If he doesn't have that part of his brain, why are we bothering?" I think her interpretation was that anyone with a disability is retarded. In defense of her, I think it was simply out of ignorance that she said this. She didn't know about the disability. So I respected the innocence or at least the will-*

**113**

*ingness to ask the question. At least she was willing to work with my son. At this time they decided he needed a full-time aide. The person who they hired was finishing her master's degree in speech. I couldn't ask for a better aide because she had the language background. She pretty much held that program together. At that time my main contact person was the speech therapist. She was resistant to anything but a whole language approach. Anytime I would make a suggestion or wanted to discuss something that might be unique to Jonathon it would start out enthusiastically but always go by the wayside.*

Things proceeded rather well in second-grade. Jonathon had a teacher who was the mother of an autistic child. This teacher offered some realistic strategies that produced progress. Mrs. Rebilog stated that things were "status quo" in third-grade. In fourth-grade, Jonathon had a new speech therapist assigned to him. Mrs. Rebilog felt that the speech therapist was excellent, but the program as a whole was not generating progress.

*I didn't see much progress. Things weren't happening that I wanted to happen. He was not participating with the kids at recess. He was not participating with the kids before school, out on the playground. That's what I had the opportunity to see. I needed this [the interaction with other students] to hap-*

*pen. Social interaction, language and phys-
ical activity go hand-in-hand. They grow
together. I felt that we were just flat-lining.
At the end of the year, the special education
teacher came to me and said, "I don't know
what else to do. We need to bring in an
expert." That was a critical turning point. I
can deal with someone telling me that they
don't know what to do. Thank goodness for
her honesty. It was the best thing that happened to us so far!*

Jonathon's program did have some significant
alterations for the next school year. A decision was made
to retain Jonathon in fourth-grade. This was something
Mrs. Rebilog had wanted to do for some time.
Additionally, a structured, specialized program, tailor-
made for Jonathon was instituted. It was an intensive
language-based program that would require more
involvement from the speech therapist. This was
something that Mrs. Rebilog had asked for since Jonathon
was in first-grade. Mrs. Rebilog felt that since she was the
only one saying this, her request was either denied or
ignored up until this point.

The district hired a consultant who specialized in
autism to help implement a program that would be fully
integrated into the routine of Jonathon's day. Additionally,
a Circle of Friends program was integrated into his
program. This is a program where Jonathon could interact
and learn social skills with non-disabled peers.

One of the crucial changes that occurred involved the
amount of collaboration between the staff people who

**115**

were working with Jonathon. The previous year there was no formalized collaboration. The collaboration piece of Jonathon's program was written into his individualized education program for the next school year. The team met every week for the first six weeks of school and then every other week.

A new one-to-one educational assistant was hired. This person had experience with individuals who had characteristics of autism.

> *The [assistant's] role changed from the aide being someone to help Jonathon through the day to someone who was given a book of steps, ideas, instructions, and was given more direction. The aide became part of the weekly meetings. She was also told by the expert that she was the one who would make or break the program.*

The role of the speech therapist also changed. She began working much more closely with the special education teacher. There was a great deal of collaboration that assisted in guiding and implementing Jonathon's educational program:

> *When the team collaborates at the meetings, the skill or the actual lesson that the fourth-grade teacher was teaching in the classroom was now incorporated into his individual speech session, as well as in the resource room. The speech teacher would actually sit in when the special education teacher was working with Jonathon to*

*bring all the three entities of his program together. So, not only was everyone working on the same skill, but they were actually working on the same academic lesson. The aide is the person who follows him through the whole thing to make sure that the continuity exists. She reminds Jonathon of the lesson through speech, and his session with the special education teacher, and how to generalize it back into the classroom. She does the trouble shooting and reports back to all team members for revisions to the program.*

Jonathon made a tremendous amount of academic and social progress this school year. The first year in fourth-grade Jonathon received a low score of 1 on the English Language Arts exam (ELA), which scores on the basis of 1 to 4 with 4 ranking highest. The second year, in fourth-grade year he went to a score of a high 3. Mrs. Rebilog reported significant progress in engagement and social interactions. She also stated that he generalized more and started to use slang and humor. These were wonderful signs of communicative and interactive improvement.

*He started to get jokes and started to use jokes . . . and is even starting to use sarcasm. I saw social and physical growth. As his language developed, his physical capabilities developed.*

Mrs. Rebilog explained as a parent what she felt she needed to do for the good of her child:

**117**

> *You gotta be a pushy pain in the ass. When it's a bad year you lose a lot. My favorite saying was "Can we freeze dry him while you people get your act together?" I'm the parent. I'm not the professional. I'm not the expert, but I can be very aggressive, if necessary. You also need to let the team members know when they are doing a good job. Let them know you appreciate their good work.*

Finally, Mrs. Rebilog spoke about having her child in an inclusionary program.

> *I know that with my son I must be part of his academic experiences on a daily basis. I must empty the book bag every day, make sure that he begins his homework, check his homework for accuracy, make sure that he is following directions, and talk to him about his day at school. Most of the time it is like pulling teeth from him, but I keep pulling. It is frustrating, tiring, boring and a pain to go through that book bag every single night, but I know that I must. I have so far been rewarded by his progress. I also maintain contact with [the educational] team members by sending notes or making phone calls, [not to his knowledge] to school about social outings and events that are happening in our life, so that they may engage him in social conversations, as well*

*as academics. This sets up nice relationships between the teachers and Jonathon. I make sure that I am available to the team for meetings at their convenience and I make sure that I attend every meeting, even if I have to lose pay from work. In my opinion, the bottom line to any child's program hinges on the support of the parent. The parent is the most influential person in the child's life, as well as the person who knows and loves that child more than anyone else does. If the parent component is not intact, I do not believe the school program can be successful. A parent of a child with an IEP cannot treat that child in the same way you treat a child who does not have an IEP. There must be additional support from home that is over and above what you would provide a typical student. From my work experiences, including my work as a tutor for the school district, I have seen students with very successful programs and students whose programs are not working so well. I have seen programs that were not working even though the parents were diligent in their support, but I have never seen a successful program when the parent was not a key player on the [educational] team.*

Sylvia Lefko has been a public school teacher for more than 20 years. She was Jonathon's fourth-grade teacher for both of the years he was in fourth-grade. The

first year Jonathon was in her class Ms. Lefko had 28
students. Six of those students were identified by the
Committee on Special Education and received special
education services. Jonathon had a one-to-one aide
assigned to him and received consultant teacher services
from a special education teacher. He also received speech
therapy. Ms. Lefko spoke about Jonathon and her
experiences working with him the first year.

> *Jonathon looked like your typical average
> fourth-grader except that his motor skills
> were a little bit off. He was a little rigid.
> His balance was a little off. He was a very
> cute little boy who was often in his own lit-
> tle world. Jonathon could appear to be
> understanding everything you were saying,
> or he might look like he was on task, but
> when you went to take a closer look at
> what was really happening, he had not a
> clue. You have to be really careful in a
> class with a lot of kids, not to overlook this.
> In instructional situations we had to move
> him so he wasn't facing a window. If he
> looked out the window he was gone. He
> was very distractible. In a situation where
> he was facing me you could just tell that he
> would "glaze over." He would kind of
> focus above my head or something very
> small and minute on his desk might get his
> attention. He spent a lot of time tuning out.
> He loved comics. I think he went into a fan-
> tasy world. It seemed like he might be cre-*

*ating elaborate little movies in his head. Jonathon was in no way a classroom behavior problem in the typical sense. He was a manageable child, but you needed a one-to-one person to re-interpret directions and keep him on task.*

But Jonathon had communication problems with her and with his classmates, Ms. Lefko said.

*Jonathon didn't initiate any real social exchange with me. He would respond with one-word answers, if I actually pushed him. I would ask him questions to help him elaborate on what he was talking about. He sometimes did volunteer and raise his hand, and he would be really proud of himself. That hand would shoot right up there, and I was always careful to call on him. He didn't relate to the other kids. He seemed to want to, but he didn't really have the language skills to do it. He would talk about things that only interested him. He never asked other children about things that interested them. He often didn't relate at all. In the playground he would run up to other kids. He would do a strange hand motion near his head . . . flap a little bit. He would sometimes play chase games with the kids. I think he would get tired and didn't want to be chased anymore. He didn't know how to tell them to stop doing*

**121**

*that, or they would tire of the game before he did. He would continue and that would annoy them. Then it would turn into a really negative situation for him.*

Very often, for students with Asperger Syndrome, communication problems lead to problems with social interaction difficulty. This was true in Jonathon's case.

*Most of the kids didn't pay much attention to him. For some of them, quite frankly, it was like he was a piece of furniture. He was someone who was just there, and they walked around him. They didn't really relate to him. If he was in a small group that was teacher-created, some of the kids would "mother" him. They would kind of take care of him and help him along. That would only happen in a group that was teacher-created. There were times when he was teased. I think that one of the characteristics of his disability was that he couldn't always tell when he was being teased. There was a very bright child in the class who was sometimes very mean and, for whatever reason, needed to put other people down. He was asking Jonathon questions like, "Are you toilet-trained?" Jonathon, being who he is, answered very seriously, "Yes, I am toilet-trained." This kid would repeat it and then a crowd of kids gathered and they were laughing at*

*Jonathon. Since the other kids were laugh-
ing the bright kid kept repeating the question, and Jonathon didn't understand what
was happening. At some point he realized
he was being laughed at. It hurt him, and
he was very upset by it and he cried. He
came in from lunch that day red-eyed and
swollen faced and really miserable. It was
heartbreaking. So I talked to the other kid
about the situation he had created for
Jonathon.*

Many times students like Jonathon receive services to
enhance programming. Coordinating these services can
be difficult. It is essential that there is communication
between everyone involved in the student's program.
Ms. Lefko, as well as Jonathon, would have benefited
greatly from better communication, coordination, and
collaboration with other staff members working with
Jonathon that first year. Ms. Lefko encountered problems
when working with other staff members the first year she
taught Jonathon.

*The one-to-one aide didn't really work out
that well. There was really no one to supervise her. The consultant teacher didn't
really come . . . maybe once in a while she
would come in the room in an off-handed,
non-structured way to say, "Well hey, how
are things going?" and then she'd leave.
She wasn't really involved in his program
at all. The speech teacher and I didn't*

*really have time to talk too much about what was going on either.*

When asked what kind of support she would have liked to work more effectively with Jonathon the first year, Ms. Lefko replied:

> *I would have liked some release time to get training where I could be trained and given some idea of what kind of program this boy needed, and what I could do as the classroom teacher to help him. I would have liked some strategies for things that I could do that would carry out what he needed and not short-change the 27 other children in the class. More importantly, Jonathon should have had a specific program in place to deal with his special needs. Children like Jonathon need "aggressive teaching" in the skills that have been identified as their deficits. His one-to-one aide, special education teacher, speech therapist, and I should have had time to discuss his needs and progress frequently during the school year.*

After the second year as Jonathon's teacher, many program changes had taken place.

> *Looking back there was a huge difference between the first year I had Jonathon and the second year I had him. The second year*

*we had a program and a team in place. There was no one to direct the one-to-one aide the first year. The aide had no training whatsoever, nor did I. The special education/consultant teacher realized she had totally failed Jonathon. Being a responsible educator she realized that she didn't know what she could do for him and asked for help. There was really no system that was in place.*

At the end of the first school year there was a meeting with Mrs. Rebilog, Ms. Lefko, the consultant teacher, and a special education administrator from the district attending. Additionally, a local expert on Asperger Syndrome was at the meeting.

*A team was established, and we all understood more clearly what Jonathon's limitations were. I was given materials to read to help me understand more.*

The second year changes were made.

*Roles were clear. Jonathon received much more special education support and the one-to-one aide knew exactly what to do. We were fastidious about making sure things didn't cloud up for her. She did record-keeping and pre-planning things for Jonathon when she wasn't working directly with him. It was really clearer what her responsibilities were.*

One of the most important features of bringing about positive change for Jonathon was the fact that there was a team approach, and a specific program was put into place.

*It gave us the structure we needed and it defined all of our roles more clearly. That made it work! It also changed the dynamics between Jonathon's mother and the rest of us. She could really see that something was happening. Finally, something that she needed to happen for a long time was finally happening. She had been the incentive to make it happen, but she could relax a little bit, because it finally was happening for her child, and she could see the changes. That made all of us feel really good.*

Additional built-in features also were instituted.

*I want to highlight something. It wasn't just the fact that there was a team. We were given time to meet. It was built into the structure on an as-needed basis. The aide, the special education teacher and myself would meet in the morning and we were compensated for our time. We met more frequently, got a lot more done, and we could invite Mrs. Rebilog to meet with us. Beyond that there were three total team meetings built in through the course of the year. Other experts came to this*

*meeting to share information. It was won-*
*derful.*

Today, Jonathon is a different boy. Ms. Lefko attributes that to the new program instituted in the second year.

*I look at Jonathon now as a fifth-grader. I*
*see him in the hall. He waves. He is very*
*comfortable. He's thriving.*

Ms. Lefko took some of the blame for Jonathon's failure. But described how instituting this program improved the second year.

*I felt terrible after the first year. I felt that I*
*had done nothing for this child. He was*
*totally lost in the classroom. I felt that*
*nothing had happened for him. The fact*
*that we retained him testifies to that. He*
*could not be just sent on. Part of that fail-*
*ure was my failure because I didn't know*
*how to address his needs at all. During the*
*second year Jonathon's needs were being*
*met by a team. It was no longer just my*
*responsibility. I felt definitely good about*
*that second year. I mean, Jonathon was the*
*success story for that year. He thrived.*

Jonathon and his mother agreed to talk about their experiences. Jonathon typically doesn't provide much detail when he is conversing. When asked if he likes school he replies, "yep." At times his mother would prompt him. Jonathon was going to a family birthday party after the interview and was wearing jeans, a shirt, vest and tie. He is a friendly boy who seems easily distracted. Throughout the interview Jonathon was pulling threads from the back of the couch. His mother asked him to stop doing it and gave him a couple of marbles to hold in his hands, but he put the marbles back. Soon after, Jonathon became distracted again and then went back to pulling threads from the couch. It was apparent that Jonathon wanted to be helpful and tried his best to answer questions. It was, however, a strain for him to answer some of the questions. Jonathon had difficulty putting his thoughts into words on one particular question. He expressed his frustration with the following response:

> *It seems I can't come up with anything. I think my brain's light bulbs burned out.*

Jonathon described the difference between his first year in Ms. Lefko's class and his second year.

> *The first year my schoolwork came out sloppy. The second year it came out more clear. In the first year, my sentences came out skinny. In the second year, they came out a lot better . . . you know, adding more details.*

Jonathon received much more support the second year. When asked if he was glad to have people to help him he replied, "uh huh." When asked what would have happen if there weren't people to help him, he said, "It would all just be a blur." When asked what that meant, he said: "It means that things are kind of fuzzy, but with them it's all clear."

What did they do to make it "more clear?"

*Well, Mrs. Smith sometimes helps me on work I didn't finish, and Ms. Torrington let's us do some writing stuff and sometimes we get to play a game. Mrs. Smith helps me add more details to my stories, and Ms. Torrington helps me on my language arts.*

What about school friends? He reported that he didn't have any the first year. He explained —

*Some of the kids thought I was weird or something. The second year I had a lot of different friends, and they liked me.*

Did his aide help him make friends? Jonathon said she did, "By showing them to me," he said.

Jonathon also talked about his aide in the lunch/recess period.

*In the second year, Ms. White got our team to play dodge ball with me. My first para [the paraprofessional from the previous year] didn't do that. Mrs. White changed her lunch schedule the second year so that she could be with me.*

Circle of Friends, a program designed to assist students with disabilities with their non-disabled peers, was instituted the second year. Jonathon talked about it.

*In the first year I didn't have Circle of Friends, but in the second year I did. We go*

*to Mrs. Duffy's [the school psychologist]
office which is behind the nurse's office. We
eat our lunch and play games.*

When asked what kind of skills he learned in Circle of Friends he said — "politeness."

Although Jonathon had some difficulty articulating his thoughts and feelings, one thing seemed apparent. His facial expressions and voice tone indicated that he was much happier the second year. Jonathon reports that as a fifth-grader he is still happy.

## Summary

It becomes clear how successful a student with a disability can be in an inclusionary learning environment, with the appropriate support, training, and programming. It also becomes clear that without the proper accommodations and supports, for the student with a disability and the educational staff, an inclusion program can be a dismal failure.

# References

Bateman, B. (1995). Who, How, and Where: Special Education's Issues in Perpetuity in *The Illusion of Full Inclusion* (eds. J.M. Kauffman & D.P. Hallahan). Austin, TX: Pro-ed Publishers

Bauwens, J., Hourcade, J., & Friend, M. (1989). Cooperative Teaching: A model for general and special education integration. *Remedial and Special Education*, 10, 17-22

Carr, M.N. (1995). A Mother's Thoughts on Inclusion in *The Illusion of Full Inclusion* (eds. J.M. Kauffman & D.P. Hallahan). Austin, TX: Pro-ed Publishers

Choate, J.S. (1997). *Successful Inclusive Teaching: Proven Ways to Detect and Correct Special Needs.* Needham Heights, MA: Allyn and Bacon

Clarke, D.D., Parry-Jones, W., Gay, B.M., & Smith, C. (1981). Disruptive incidents in secondary school classrooms: a sequence analysis approach. *Oxford Review of Education*, 7 (2), 111-132

Crawford, J., Brockel. B., Schauss, S., & Miltenberger, R. (1992). A comparison of methods for the functional assessment of stereotypic behavior. *The Journal of the Association for Persons with Severe Handicaps*, 17, 77-86

Dipalma M.F. (1995). *Inclusive Education in New York City: Strategies for Achieving Success.* NY, New York:

New York State Developmental Disabilities Planning Council

Donnellan, A., Mirenda, P., Mesaros R., & Fassbender, L. (1984). Analyzing the communicative functions of aberrant behavior. *The Journal of the Association for Persons with Severe Handicaps*, 9, 201-212

Downing. J.E., Ryndak, D.L., & Clark, D. (2000). Paraeducators in inclusive classrooms. *Reading and Special Education*, 21(3), 171-181

Feldman, C. (1994, October 7). Inclusion of disabled. The Schenectady Gazette, p. A 2

Fisher, D. & McGregor, G. (1996). A Framework for Evaluating State and Local *Policies for Inclusion*. Issue Brief

French, N.K., & Chopra, R. (1999). Parent perspectives on the roles of paraprofesionals. *The Journal of the Association for Persons with Severe Handicaps*, 24, 259-272

Freschi, D. (1999). Guidelines for working with one-to-one aides. *Teaching Exceptional Children*, March/April

Fuchs, D., Fuchs, L.S., Bahr, M.W., Fernstrom, P., & Stecker, P.M. (1990). Prereferral intrervention: A prescriptive approach. *Exceptional Children*, 56(6), 493-513

Gallagher, J.J. (1994). The Pull of Societal Forces on Special Education. *The Journal of Special Education*, Vol. 27. 521-530

Giangreco, M.F. & Putnam, & Putnam, J.W. (1991). Supporting the education of students with severe disabilities in regular education environments. *In Critical Issues in the Lives of People with Severe Disabilities* (eds. L.H. Meyer, C.A. Peck & L. Brown). Baltimore, MD: Paul H. Brookes Publishing Co.

Graden, J.L. & Bauer, A.M. (1994). Using a Collaborative Approach to Support Students and Teachers in Inclusive Classrooms in Curriculum Considerations in Inclusive Classrooms: Facilitating Learning for all Students (eds. S. Stainback & W. Stainback). Baltimore, MD: Paul H. Brookes Publishing Co.

Hardman, M.L., McDonnell, J., & McDonnell, A. (1989). The inclusive neighborhood school: Educating students with severe disabilities in the least restrictive environment. Manuscript submitted for publication

Heckman, M., & Rike, C. (1994). Westwood early learning center. *Teaching Exceptional Children*, Winter, 30-35

Huefner, D.S. (1988). The consulting teacher model: Risks and Opportunities. *Exceptional Children*, 54, 403-424

Johnson, L.J., Pugach, M.C., & Hammitte, G. (1988). Barriers to effective special education consultation. *Remedial and Special Education*. 9(6), 41-47

Joynt, R.J. & Blackwell, R.R. (1980). *Mainstreaming: What to Expect . . . What to Do*. Johnstown, PA: Mafex Associates, Inc. Publishers

Kauffman, J.M. & Hallahan, D P. (1995). From Main-streaming to Collaborative Consultation in *The Illusion of Full Inclusion* (eds. J.M. Kauffman & D.P. Hallahan). Austin, TX: Pro-ed Publishers

Kauffman, J.M. & Hallahan, D.P. (1995). Full Inclusion in Historical Context in *The Illusion of Full Inclusion* (eds. J.M. Kauffman & D.P. Hallahan). Austin, TX: Pro-ed Publishers

McGregor, G., & Vogelsberg, R.T. (1998). *Inclusive Schooling Practices: Pedagogical and Research Foundations.* Baltimore, MD. Paul H. Brookes Publishing Co., Inc.

Miller, L. (1990). The regular education initiative and school reform: Lessons from the mainstream. *Remedial and Special Education*, 11(3), 17-22

Miller, T.L., & Sabatino, D. (1978). An evaluation of the teacher consultation model as an approach to mainstreaming. *Exceptional Children*, 45(2), 86-91

Mueller, P.H. (1997). A study in the roles, training needs, and support of Vermont's paraeducators. (Doctoral dissertation, University of Vermont, 1997) Dissertation Abstracts International. 9970545

Mueller, P.H., & Murphy F.V. (2001). Determining when a student requires paraeducator support. *The Council for Exceptional Children* July/August, 22-27

O'Brien, J., & Forest, M. (1989). *Action for Inclusion: How to Improve Schools by Welcoming Children with Spe-*

*cial Needs into Regular Classrooms*. Toronto, Canada: Inclusion Press

Patterson, G.R., & Bank, L. (1986). Bootstrapping your way in the nomological thicket. *Behavioral Assessment*, 8, 49-73

Pickett, A.L. (1999). Strengthening and supporting teacher/provider-paraeducator teams: Guidelines for paraeducator roles, supervision, and preparation. New York: National Resource Center for Paraprofessionals in Education and Related Services, Center for Advanced Study in Education, Graduate Center, City University of New York

Raywide, M.A. (1993). Finding time for collaboration. *Educational Leadership*, vol. 51(1).

Robinson, V. (1990, Fall). Regular education initiative: Debate on the current state and future promise of a new approach to educating children with disabilities. Counterpoint, p.5

Salisbury, C.L. & McGregor, G. (2002). The administrative climate and context of inclusive elementary schools. *The Council for Exceptional Children* Vol. 68 No.2 pp. 259-274

Sapon-Shevin, M. (1994). Celebrating Diversity Creating Community in *Curriculum Considerations in Inclusive Classrooms: Facilitating Learning for All Students* (eds. S. Stainback & W. Stainback). Baltimore, MD: Paul H. Brookes Publishing Co.

Smith, M. & Misra, A. (1992). A comprehensive management system for students in regular classrooms. *The Elementary School Journal*, 92, (3) 353-372

Stainback, S. & Stainback, W. (1994). Toward Inclusive Classrooms in *Curriculum Considerations in Inclusive Classrooms: Facilitating Learning for all Students* (eds. S. Stainback & W. Stainback). Baltimore, MD: Paul H. Brookes Publishing Co.

Stainback, S., Stainback, W. & Moravec, J. (1994). Using Curriculum to Build Inclusive Classrooms in *Curriculum Considerations in Inclusive Classrooms: Facilitating Learning for all Students* (eds. S. Stainback & W. Stainback). Baltimore, MD: Paul H. Brookes Publishing Co.

Tilton, L. (1997). *Inclusion a Fresh Look: Practical strategies to help all students succeed.* Shorewood, MN: Covington Cove Publications

Vandover, T. (1996). *The Inclusion Guide for Handling Chronically Disruptive Behavior.* Manhattan, KS: The Master Teacher, Inc. Publisher

Walker, H., & Sylwester, R. (1991). Where is school along the path to prison? *Educational Leadership*, September. 14-16

Will, M. (1984). Educating Children with Learning Problems: A Shared Responsibility. *Exceptional Children*, Vol. 52, 411-415

# References

Wood, J.W. (1992). *Adapting Instruction for Mainstreamed and At-Risk Students.* New York, NY: Merril Publishing Company

Zimmerman, B.F. (1998). Classroom Disruption: Educational Theory as Applied to Perception and Action in Regular and Special Education. In A. Rotatori, J. Schwenn & S. Burkhardt (Eds.), *Advances in Special Education*, pp. 77-98, Greenwich, CT.: JAI Press Inc.

Zimmerman, B.F. (2000). *On Our Best Behavior: Positive Behavior Management Strategies for the Classroom.* Horsham, PA: LRP Publications